LIVING

SINGLE

Pastor Deana Gordon

American Heritage Talking Dictionary; CD-ROM, Third edition; Houghton Mifflin Company © 1995 by Inso Corporation. All rights reserved.
Anticipation, Gospel Music Workshop of America National Mass Choir, Live In Indianapolis, V. Michael McKay
Back Cover Photo Credit; Dorothy Jarrett
Printing, OMNI PublishXPress, Nashville, TN
Scripture quotations noted The Message are from The Message: The New Testament Psalms and Proverbs Copyright © 1993, 1994, 1995, 1996 by Eugene H. Peterson. All rights reserved.
Scripture quotations noted KJV are from the King James Version of the bible
Scripture quotations noted AMP are from the Amplified Bible Copyright© 1987, by the Zondervan Corporation and The Lockman Foundation. Used by permission. All rights reserved.
Scripture quotations noted NIV are from the Holy Bible: New International Version. Copyright© 1973, 1978, 1984 by International Bible Society; Used by permission. All rights reserved.
Scripture quotations not noted are from the NAS. Updated New American Standard Bible, Copyright © 1960, 1962, 1963, 1968, 1971, 1973, 1975, 1977, 1995 by The Lockman Foundation. Used by permission. All rights reserved.
Webster's Dictionary, Merriam Webster,Inc.© 1995. All rights reserved.
Word Records, 1995, Lord I'm Available, Thompson Community Choir.

Dedication

This book is dedicated to every single person that is determined to live a rich and full single life that honors God. May God be glorified in all that you do!

Special Thanks

Thank you, to all the men of God who shared their testimonies with me. Your experiences gave insight from a necessary perspective that will bless the lives of many men who desire to live wholeheartedly for God.

TABLE OF CONTENTS

Introduction
Living Single

If your experience has been any thing like mine, then you learned about living the single life from your peers or what you saw on television. The expectations I developed for my single life began at a time when I was very impressionable particularly during my formative adolescent and teenage years.

At that season of my life, I was a Days of Our Lives Soap Opera fanatic! I just knew that one day my Beau was going to come riding by on his big shiny motor cycle, leather bound, with his hair blowing in the wind and whisk me (his Hope) away with him.

But then again, I believe that my vivid imagination was nurtured earlier during kindergarten reading time. As stories were read to me I fantasized of living the fairy tale of Cinderella and Prince Charming. Like so many other young girls I just wanted what everybody else wanted. Come on, it has to be a good thing if everybody wants it, right? In my mind I guess I assumed that the popular thing just had to be the right thing. Go figure!

It took more than a minute, but I finally realized that the popular thing is not always the right thing and the right thing is not always popular! Now when I look back over my life I am glad that I did not earn all of the benchmarks it took to obtain popularity and acclaim among my peers.

Most discuss *"peer pressure"* as an issue that is far beneath contemporary adults. Let me dispel that untruth. Peer pressure is deceptively hidden with adults under the expression, *"keeping up with Joneses"*. Both are really the same game of intense competition— same game but the latter has higher aims. The pressure that adults feel because "she" got married first or "he" got a job making a better salary are just as real as the teenager who does not have the latest pair of sneakers. It does not matter if we are twenty-one, thirty-five, forty or even seventy-five. Adults are not exempt from the pressures of their peers.

Every one wants to belong and feel accepted. Belonging and being accepted are just a couple of the basic needs of life. The sad fact is that many of us have regrettably done whatever was necessary to meet those basic needs regardless of how superficial the act and unfulfilling the result.

I grew up in the church, as I am sure many of you reading this book did too! But to my detriment topics that would nurture me spiritually as a single woman were forbidden territory. Dating, marriage, and the S—word (SEX), yes S-E-X, S-E-X, S-E-X, were not part of the Sunday School curriculum. No, no, no, you just did not talk about topics like that! So, I was basically left to guess and conform so that I would fit into the mainstream. I had no idea at the time but the mainstream had a strong current that flowed directly into the ways of the world and very far away from God.

Like most of us I am sure you only heard the bare minimum about the facts of life. That bare minimum for most of us was only enough to spark an interest to drive us to pursue answers from unreliable sources. Hey, inquiring minds want to know! That 's just the way it is. But, following bad information has terrible consequences that can last a lifetime.

If you heard anything about sexuality maybe you heard the story about the birds and the bees? Maybe you heard about the stork. Sex is only to make babies! Maybe your story was filled with creative names for body parts. No dating, until you are sixteen! It's just puppy love! Your skirt is not long enough! No make-up! When you have sex you get pregnant, so don't do it. But, if you must, use birth control???? Go talk to your daddy! Go ask your mother! Ask your sister! A man has got to do what a man has got to do, but make sure you marry a nice girl. Does any of this sound familiar?

We are destroyed because of the lack of knowledge! As a very young, precocious and impressionable girl the enemy made sure that I learned a distorted truth (lies) from my elementary classmates, and the bathroom walls. My high school and college classmates always felt privileged to wisely expound from their "*plethora* of *meaningful intimate experiences*". The few peers I had at church were just as lost and misinformed as me. They were just as blind and we were all walking into the live minefield of life with the potential for a deadly explosion at anytime.

But as it goes, when we know better then we do better. The sad thing is that the future of so many are destroyed daily, sacred treasures are carelessly sacrificed, and innocent souls are wounded because of the absence of biblical truths about the way God desires for us to live as "*single saints*". Therefore, the awful cycles continue—pregnancy after pregnancy, divorce after divorce, disease after disease, and broken experience after broken experience! Please, declare today that the cycle of ignorance will end with you!

In this fast paced society people are often mocked and ridiculed for speaking the truth of God's word and living according to the example of Jesus the Christ who died without any apprehension as a thirty-three year old virgin.

The enemy cunningly attempts to make us think that it is easier to be just like everybody else. We must dare to be different as we change the world by our living example that boldly proves what is that good, perfect and acceptable will of God. The bible exhorts us to "be ye separate and come out from among them". God has called the body of Christ to be a beacon of light in this dark world. As single men and women of God we must assume our positions!

Anyone can be just like everyone else, but a person that really loves Jesus will dare to be different no matter what the cost. My prayer is that you will grasp this knowledge so that your Christian journey is both fruitful and productive. Parents this book will help you to minister to your children. Married couples, you will be given answers to problems that should have been addressed before the wedding. Living Single will enable you to empower singles in their walk of faith and holiness. You will soon discover that being single is much more than just a place of waiting!

1.   How has your early education or mis-education of sexuality affected your life?

2.   What were some of the greatest influences that contributed to your present knowledge base about living single?

3.   If you are a parent or hope to be a parent some day what would you like your children to know about living single that you did not know?

4.   How has your life been affected by bad choices that others in society make about their own single lifestyle?

5.   In your opinion do your attitudes and behaviors reflect a godly character that will compel others to duplicate your example? Why or why not?

WANTED:

JUBILANT SINGLE CHRISTIAN!!!

The Single Person

In order to function with any degree of success as a single person we must first identify who qualifies as the "*Single*" person. Each of us has a variety of experiences in our lives that we think "*amends*" the criteria and obligations for the category of singleness as it pertains to Christianity. Nevertheless, there are three types of people who fit the single category—the widowed, the divorced and those who have never been married. The bible is filled with single people that we can identify with. I took the liberty of mentioning just a few.

2Kings allows us to read about a dramatic moment in the life of a widowed woman left to raise her sons and deal with bringing closure to her family's unfinished business.

2King 4:1 Now a certain woman of the wives of the sons of the prophets cried out to Elisha, "Your servant my husband is dead, and you know that your servant feared the Lord; and the creditor has come to take my two children to be his slaves."

The book of Ruth is a narrative that allows us to experience the anxiety of three widowed women beginning again without the support of their husbands who defined their identity and served as the financial support for the family.

Ruth 1:3-7 Then Elimelech, Naomi's husband died and she was left with her two sons. They took for themselves Moabite women as wives; the name of the one was Oprah and the name of the other Ruth....Then, both Mahlon and Chilion also died, and the woman was bereft of her two children and her husband. So they departed from the place where she was, and her two daughters-in-law with her; and they went on the way to return to the land of Judah.

The Gospel of John introduces us to the Samaritan Woman whose life displays the stress and frustrations of a divorced woman attempting to quench her spiritual thirst with alleged natural water as she tirelessly looked for love in all the wrong places.

John 4:17-18 The woman answered and said, " I have no husband". Jesus said unto her, "You have correctly said, I have no husband": For you have had five husbands; and the one whom you now have is not your husband", "this you have said truly."

The book of Judges unveils the disappointing story of the life of a man called Samson who was controlled by sensuality. Samson is remembered as a single man who had it all and almost lost it all for the lust of women, especially the woman named Delilah.

Judges 16: 1+4+18 Now Samson went to Gaza and saw a harlot there and went in to her. After this it came to pass that he loved a woman in the valley of Sorek whose name was Delilah. When Delilah saw that he had told her all that was in his heart, she went and called the lords of the Philistines saying, "Come up once more, for he has told me all that is in his heart." Then the lords of the Philistines came up to her and brought the money in their hands.

Some theologians suggest that Paul was once married because a man has to be married to be part of the Sanhedrin council, of which Paul was once a part. But we know that he describes himself as a single person, in his responsive letter to the church at Corinth.

1Cor. 7:7-8 Yet, I wish that all men were even as I myself am. However, each man has his own gift from God, one in this manner and another that. But I say to the unmarried and to the widows that it is good for them to remain even as I.

The gospel of Luke depicts the story of a single woman with a questionable history. The portrait of her life suggests that she lived a sinful single life since she had no revelation of Jesus. But once she met Jesus Him her life was forever changed and devoted to the Lord. She presented a devotional gift of an alabaster box to her Lord that was usually part of a dowry for her husband to be.

Luke 7:36-38 Now one of the Pharisees was requesting Him to dine with them, and He entered the Pharisees house and reclined at the table, And there was a woman in the city who was a sinner when she learned that He was reclining at the table in the Pharisees' house, she brought an alabaster vial of perfume and standing behind Him at His feet, weeping, she began to wet His feet with her tears, and kept wiping them with the hair of her head, and kissing His feet and anointing them with the perfume.

The book of Genesis records the story of a young, attractive and anointed man that loved God. He was committed to truth and integrity because of his relationship with God. But the married woman where he worked did not understand nor desire to honor his commitment. There are men who can identify with this young man's struggle with striving to live holy surrounded by unholy women who want them to fulfill their most recent unrighteous fantasy.

Gen. 39: 1+3+7 + 9 Now Joseph had been taken down to Egypt; and Potiphar, an Egyptian officer of Pharaoh, the captain of the bodyguard, bought him from the Ishmaelite, who had taken him down there. Now his master saw that the Lord was with him and how the Lord caused all that he did to prosper in his hand. It came about after these events that his master's wife looked with desire at Joseph, and said, "Lie with me."...And Joseph responded, "How then could I do this great evil and sin against God?"

All of these *"people"* mentioned were single.   They are not just characters in a book with imagined feelings and desires. These were real people with real feelings. They all lived during a different time and in a different place but the fact remains that they were still single. They all experienced the same full range of human emotions that single people deal with on a daily basis. It was a different time and different place but there is much that can be gleaned from both their achievements and their mistakes. Each person had to deal with overcoming temptations and struggles with making the right decision as they endeavored to live for God just like single Christians today.

In order to move forward in the path that God has predestined for you life you must first honestly acknowledge where you are to understand where you are going. Where are you? Who are you? What do you really want? Why do you really want it?

You may have always been classified as single or maybe your life has had a turn of events that brought you to a place that you thought that you would never visit again. Whatever the situation—single is single. Now ask the Lord this question, where do we go from here?

1.   Does your present or past situation resemble any of the single persons mentioned? Can you identify with their pain and uncertainty?

2.   Can you identify more with the strong desire to fulfill lust or with the others who desire a deep devoted relationship with the Lord?

3.   Based on the brief descriptions given what is the difference between The Samaritan woman and Mary? Read each noted section of scripture further if necessary.

4.   What is the difference between Joseph and Samson? Are you more of a Samson or a Joseph?

5.   What are the similarities and differences between the widowed woman in 2Kings, and Ruth, Naomi and Oprah?

6.   Potiphar's wife asked Joseph to "lie with her". Women, have you ever been Potiphar's wife, a woman of seduction? What lie did you want your Joseph to help you create?

7.   Delilah saw that Samson had told her what was in his heart and then she took from him and Samson was left weak. Have you ever been Delilah? What did you take? What did you gain? What did your Samson lose because of you?

" IN MY SINGLENESS JESUS HAS GIVEN ME EVERTHING I NEED"

SINGLE AND COMPLETE

We encounter inevitable challenges as we live single in this American society especially when living single is considered living an incomplete lifestyle. Well, wait a second! The world has set a standard that subliminally suggests that temporary attachments are acceptable while living single. That sugges-tion supposedly upgrades our position in the lifestyles of the "*single and searching*".

Somebody, anybody is better than no one at all. (Whatever!) I can do bad all by myself! Everyone loves the lifestyle of the bodacious bachelor or the beautiful bacheloret. As long as we have the option to pick and choose, our calendar is filled with dates, and our little black book is at maximum capacity we are considered to be living large. Wrong again!

The world is decorated with a ready welcome for "*couples*" at every turn. Every restaurant is designed with tables for "*two*". I've never heard of anyone giving away tickets for "*one*" to the Bahamas. There are always tickets for at least "*two*". Then you're forced to take someone along that you really do not want to be bothered with or forfeit the trip.

It is forbidden to think of going out alone, right??? Don't think of going to the movies alone —even though talking is supposed to be minimal. Go figure!

I remember sometime ago I dared to go out alone! I was eating breakfast at a restaurant. The hostess asked me how many were in my party. I said one. Feeling insecure, I quietly thought, "some party". She looked at me with disappointment in her face. She couldn't believe that I had ventured to eat alone and she proceeded to empathize with me by saying, "I'm sorry Sugar!" I just smiled and thought to myself, "Right, thanks a lot!" "You are really helping me here!" "Will you just take my order and bring me my food!"

Every other commercial on television sends strong messages and innuendos that are not supportive of living the "*Single Christian Lifestyle*". The world's expectation, and desires have sadly been adopted as our own. Hollywood, the music industry and the media lead us to believe that one is the loneliest number that we will ever know.

Let's make the record clear! One is a whole number. One is not half of a whole. One is a whole number. One is not lonely but alone. Mathematically one may be less than two but as it pertains to individuality, one stands sure all by itself.

When God created man and woman He did not create us so that our creative ability and learning capacity was contingent on anyone else. When God created both male and female He created each equipping us with everything that was necessary to live a successful life. As born again believer's we have everything that we need to live an abundant life.

2Peter 1:1-4 Grace and peace be multiplied to you in the knowledge of God and Jesus our Lord; seeing that His divine power has granted to us every thing pertaining to life and godliness, through the true knowledge of Him who called us by His own glory and excellence. For by these He granted to us His precious and magnificent promises, so that by them you may become partakers of the divine nature, having escaped the corruption that is in the world by lust.

God did not create us as incomplete persons. Doing so would give us an innate desire to depend on another human to complete our identity. I am who the Lord says I am. The Lord says that I am a priest, and a Son of God. I am a Daughter of God. I am only who the Lord says I am! (Gal. 4:6-7, Luke 13: 16, Rev. 1:5-6)

People who see themselves as half will only attract another half. An incomplete creation would innately prompt us to live a co-dependent lifestyle. When we live thinking that we are incomplete we live a life that accepts a lower standard of living rather than the high but obtainable standard that God has preordained for our lives.

Eph. 2:10 For we are his workmanship, created in Christ Jesus unto good works, which God prepared beforehand so that we would walk in them.

We must expect the best! This world has a way giving us whatever we will accept just to get by. We must demand more for ourselves. People who describe themselves as incomplete usually spend most of their lives waiting rather than actively moving in the pursuit of purpose and destiny.

After years of life pass by people who believe they are incomplete usually end up lifeless throwing around phrases like, *"what if I had"*, *"maybe I should have"* or *"I could have."* People who see themselves as incomplete have to be prodded and pumped just to begin to live. They usually have goals that are contingent on the actualization of someone else's goals. It's always if they, then I will. Haven't you heard it before? Consequently, they are often intimidated and or threatened by the success of someone else that has taken the initiative to move forward in their purpose.

A person that knows they are complete rests at the opposite end of the spectrum. They see things totally different. They proudly proclaim that I am what the Lord says I am. They are not diligently searching for affirmation from others. They well know that their sufficiency is in the Lord (2Cor. 3: 5) which makes any and everything good possible in their lives.

Compliments given to a person who knows they are complete is but a mere recognition of what the complete person already knows. Before you go there, it's not called "conceit". It's called CONFIDENCE! It's also called APPRECIATING what God created! When you know that you are complete you are not floored when the opinions of others about you are different from your own because you are secure in who you are. When others fail to notice your new outfit or recent achievement it will not make or break your day!

Women! When you doubt who you are in the Lord the slightest bit of attention will not take you on a quick trip to cloud nine nor will an oversight take you to sorrows valley. Men! When you know who you are in the Lord it will not be so easy to manipulate you by stroking your ego!

Gen 1:27 So God created man in His own image, God created He him; male and female created He them.

God loves each of us very much. We are each a unique masterpiece! He wanted us to be just like Him. There is no one else like Him and there is no one else like you! When you are not confident about whom you are in the Lord your response to the previous statement is probably, "That's a good thing the world is better off!" But, when you appreciate your uniqueness you can celebrate the awesome demonstration of God's creative power in you! Hey, take a look around! We are all different! None of us are just alike! But, no one wants to be different. Well, I'm sorry folk that's just the way that God created us to be. Believe it or not it's really okay. As a matter of fact it is WONDERFUL!!!!!!!!

We must be careful. A thankless attitude about our individuality is an insult toward God's ability. Complaining about what God created you to be is like saying, "God could have done better". Beauty is in the eye of the beholder and when God finished creating you He stood back, smiled proudly, stuck out His chest and said, AWESOME! God created us with just what we needed to be the people that He has called us to be. He designed us so that we could finish the purpose and plan for our lives successfully. Everything about us was uniquely designed so that we could be victorious in every battle and accomplish every task that lies in the pathway of our destiny.

Now if you have mishandled the "*art work*" so that you no longer look like the original then that my dear will require more work on our part. Nevertheless, that does not mean that you did not start off wonderful. Anyway, in spite of your situation you are still accepted and loved by God!

I used to complain because my shoe size is ten and not seven. I complained because my hair was not curly but coarse and kinky (without the perm) and I am big-boned not short and petite. And then one day I recognized that I could be walking around with no feet and my feet are in correct proportion with my body. With the experiences that I have had with my hair, if it was soft and curly it would probably be gone by now. And my ministry responsibilities put my large legs and strong arms to good use. We must never forget that God is God and He knew just what He was doing when He uniquely designed us!

> **Ps 139:14** I will give thanks to you, for I am fearfully and wonderfully made.

There is no one that can do, what I do like I can do it. I am the best and the only me. Let's say that again! There is no one that can do what I do like I can do it. I am the best "me" and the only "me".

When a congregation invites me to their church they do not want anyone else they want me. If I show up and present myself as someone that I am not I will cheat them out of the gift of me that only I can give. A request for me means that you like the way that I do it—not the person down the street. When we try to be someone else we are doing nothing but offering a cheap imitation of the original. There is no one that can be me but me. I am the single, original, and the best Deana Gordon there is! Now you say it!

I am the single, the original and the best _____ _____
there is!   (your name)

REPEAT IT UNTIL YOU BELIEVE IT!

Blessed be the name of the Lord! I am so special to the Lord that He did not want anyone to be like me. I am the only me He created! I am priceless to my Father.

Our individual talents, gifts and abilities came wrapped up in a package called ME. We are not like some toy where the batteries are not included or the accessories are sold separately. As born again believers God has given us everything that we need.

1.   What societal subliminal messages have you attempted to meet or maintain in your life as a single person?

2.   What messages do you agree or disagree with that are present in today's videos, television and movies?

3.   What messages can be derived from an active dating schedule?

4.   Do you feel uncomfortable about going out alone? If so, what are you going to do to change the way you feel?

5.   As a single person do you feel complete or incomplete? What can you do to change or maintain your standing?

6.   Read 2Peter1:4. How does this scripture apply to your life?

7.   If you could rate the level of expectation for yourself from one to ten what would it be? (Ten being always expecting the best and one being extremely low expectation) Is there room for improvement? What's your plan for improvement?

8.   God thinks you are wonderful! How do you feel about yourself? Look in the mirror and write down what you see and how you feel about what you see. Do you find it is easier to say something positive or something negative? Why?

Pray this prayer:

Lord I thank you because you love me unconditionally. I thank you Lord because you love me just the way I am. You love me enough to want me to be the best person that I can be and you are still pleased with me even in my process of becoming.

Lord I recognize that there are some areas of my life that I am insecure and uncertain about. Lord right now I submit those areas to you. I trust you to bring me to a place of certainty about who I am and who you created me to be. I thank you because I know that I am always loved and beautiful in your sight. In Jesus name Amen.

AM I FULLY COMMITED?

SINGLE COMMITMENT

1Cor 7:32 ...One who is unmarried is concerned about the things of the Lord, how he may please the Lord.

In many instances a strong desire to be involved in an intimate relationship may cause us to assume responsibilities and attempt to meet expectations that a single person is exempt from.

The problem is that we are usually in search of security and affirmation from others that can only be discovered in God. Consequently, we find ourselves wrapped up in several different relationships with shallow short-term commitments. So, just as our commitment wavers so do our feelings of security and affirmation. When we find contentment in our Heavenly Father we will find that place of peace and security that will always be present regardless of who comes or goes in our lives.

As single saints our devotion and full commitment must be to our Lord. There are many single people who are devoted mind, body, and soul to relationships outside of God's will. As a result, the responsibilities of a wife or husband are assumed that *"a single person is not obligated to fulfill"*.

I want to relieve some of you today from doing all that unnecessary work! He that is married cares for the things that are of the world, and how he may please his wife. She that is married cares for the things of the world and how she may please her husband.

Single man it is not your responsibility to pay another woman's mortgage, nor is it your responsibility to buy groceries to feed her children. Who will her children call daddy next month? Who's fooling whom? Don't get angry because you've been used. No one uses us unless we allow ourselves to be used. Why did you really do what you did anyway? Was it because you cared or was it because you were trying to get in good?

You are not the man of the house unless you are married to the woman in the house. When you become the man of the house you can assume those responsibilities. Remember the words of wisdom from your parents.

Pro. 6:20-24 (NIV) My son, keep your father's commands and do not forsake your mother's teaching. Bind them upon your heart forever; fasten them around your neck. When you walk, they will guide you; when you sleep, they will watch over you; when you awake, they will speak to you for these commands are a lamp, this teaching is a light, and corrections of discipline are the way to life, keeping you from the smooth tongue of the wayward wife.

Single woman listen to me. You do not have to furnish his wardrobe. You do not have to do his laundry, clean his house, have dinner on the table, and neither must you have his bath water ready when he gets off from work! Are you crazy? Without a covenant agreement that is "*honored by God*" and "*the law*" you are simply his maid. Why would he buy the cow when he can get the *milk* for free?

Stepping over boundaries will open the door up for misplaced hopes and broken dreams. Who will you play house with next if that relationship does not last? SHE IS NOT YOUR WIFE!!!! HE IS NOT YOUR HUSBAND!!! Wait! The joy of ministering to your mate will all come soon enough. You will have the pleasure of doing all those wonderful things later! Please, do yourself a favor now. Wait until you are married before you act married! A single person cares for the things of the Lord. There are many other things that you can do to express your "*Christian love*".

Pro. 4:7 (KJV) Wisdom is the principal thing; therefore get wisdom; and with all thy getting get understanding.

As a single woman you should not ask a man that you are not married to, to assume the role of a spouse in her life. Trust God to help you do what you cannot do for yourself. It is better to depend on your parents or another morally reliable source, if necessary than to become vulnerable in a temporary relationship. I do believe that there are things that men by nature are better built physically to do than women and in those cases it is acceptable to call on men for assistance in that given area. In the same instance it also fair for a man to ask a woman to do things for him that are typically the strengths of a woman.

However, making a minor household repair or lifting a heavy item does not give the single man the right to expect a "*wife's return*" of expression from the single woman he has befriended. Neither should a single woman expect a "*husband's return*" for her random act of kindness. An act of kindness is a privilege not an **I.O.U.** Depend on God to do what He has already promised that He would do. A significant other should never take God's place in our lives married or single.

Exodus 34:14 (Amp) For you shall worship no other god; for the Lord whose name is jealous, is a jealous (impassioned) God.

When we have found a place of rest in the providence of God we allow Him alone to be our comforter, helper and our provider. Once you have allowed Him to be the God of your life you will never want another substitute. No one can love you like God can.

God's jealousy can be compared to that of a husband whose wife has been adulterous. God does not want to compete with anyone for your love and attention. When we seek other sources outside of our commitment to God we have violated the fidelity of our relationship with Him. Someone else has become our Lord.

We live in a society that bases love on things. Don't let the standard of society fool you. Society suggests that if you give something tangible then that is supposed to be accurately measure the depth of your love. The greater the dollar value of the tangible thing the greater the love! Yea right! I don't think so! That would mean if I have nothing to give then I have no love. Actually, if we are not giving "*things*" then that could be demonstrating how much I really love you and how much I want you to trust God. It excites me to know that I am kept by God!!!!! Maybe that is the reason why after the "*honeymoon period*", of relationships, when the gifts stop coming, the love is thought to be gone as well.

It is both accepted and expected for us to be a blessing to our fellow brother or sister in Christ as long as we expect nothing in return. If we expect something in return for our kindness then what we gave was not a gift but merely "*an exchange*".

Check your motives. Here is a good gauge for your giving. Our actions must consistently be the same all the way across the board. Would your kind behavior be the same for any other *brother* or *sister* in Christ? As a sister would you be just as *kind* to another sister? If you are a brother would you be just as *kind* to another brother? Kindness knows no gender! True love is not partial. Our love for the Lord should always motivate us to express love toward one another. We should not display eros (erotic love) to our brothers and sisters but agape (unconditional love) and phileo (friendly love) toward one another.

As singles our first commitment is to the Lord. Believe it or not that is a wonderful place to be. God created us to worship and adore Him. Marriage is not a mandate of creation but loving relationships between one another is what He commands. However, without first having a commitment to the Lord we cannot lovingly relate to one another. Our vertical relationship with the Lord will dictate our horizontal relationships with everyone else. That is the way of the cross!

Matthew 22:37-3(KJV) Thou shalt love the Lord your God with all your heart and with all your soul and with all of your mind. This is the first and the greatest commandment and the second is like unto it, thou shalt love thy neighbor as thyself.
1John 4:20-21 If someone says, "I love God", and hates his brother, he is a liar; for the one who does not love his brother, whom he   has seen, cannot love God whom he has not seen. And this commandment we have from Him, that the one who loves God should love his brother also.

God did not say, *"I created you to worship me and get married".* God created us to worship Him and be in fellowship with Him. God did not save us so that we could preach or operate in spiritual gifts. God saved us so that we could be in relationship with Him. We were created to bring Him pleasure.

Col. 1:16 For by Him all things were created, both in heaven and on the earth, visible and invisible, whether thrones or dominions or rulers or authorities, all things have been created through Him and for Him.
Lev. 26:9-12 So, I will turn toward you and make you fruitful and multiply you and I will confirm My covenant with you. You will eat the old supply and clear out the old because of the new. Moreover, I will make My dwellings among you, and you shall be my people.

Being single and being married are both great ways to glorify God. Each lifestyle has different dynamics with the same expected end—to glorify God. A husband honors and glorifies God as he provides for his family. God created the man to be a *"protector"* and a *"provider".* The husband is the head of the household and he must protect and provide for his family. He honors God by being an example of both practical and spiritual leadership in his household.

The wife honors and worships God as she submits to her husband. In the Greek the word Elucidation means that wives are to give their husbands the same unquestionable absolute submission that they give Christ. In other words, when a wife submits to her husband she is in order and worshipping the Christ.

The woman glorifies God when she operates as the *"nurturer"* of the family that God has created her to be. The wife must cultivate and develop an environment in the home that influences the condition of the home so that they are favorable for each family member's character. Both the husband and wife must love God first. However, one way they express their love for God is when they faithfully walk in the assigned role that God has given them in their family.

Ephesians 5:22-26+28-29 Wives, be subject to your own husbands, as to the Lord. For the husband is the head of the wife, as Christ also is the head of the church and gave Himself up for her so that He might sanctify her, having cleansed her by the washing of water with the word. So husbands also ought to also love their own wives as their own bodies. He who loves his own wife loves himself; for no one ever hated his own his own flesh, but nourished and cherishes it, just as Christ also does the church.

As singles we are totally committed unto the Lord. The focus of our interests are not split. I have spoken to many men and women who are now married. They have told me that they did not realize that there was *"blessedness"* in being single. During their season of singleness they exerted all of their energy into looking to find *Mr. Right* or they were busy *"playing the field"*. Now troublesome times immediately turn into frantic failures in their marriage.

The problem is that neither marriage partner had a real relationship with the Lord before the wedding. If their commitment to the Lord were established during their season of singleness, they would be much stronger during times of crisis in their marriage.

When a man and woman are married, private golden moments of intimacy with the Lord must be carefully planned and scheduled because of the preoccupation that married couples have with running the household, and dealing with varied family matters.

As singles we must take advantage of the time that God has given us with Him right now! Your season of singleness should be one of the greatest times of your life. Please do not allow the enemy to rob you of what God has in place to richly bless you. Seize this moment in time that the Lord has given you. Take every opportunity to become more deeply involved with the Lord. Build your foundation now not later. Allow Jesus to be the lover of your soul. Let Him love you like no one else can. Allow Him to fill that empty space in you that is reserved for Him. Attempting to fill that place with anything else is like running water in a bathtub without out plugging the drain. The water occupies *some* of the space in tub for only a moment but the tub always drains empty.

Matt. 6:33 Seek ye first the kingdom of God and His righteousness and then all these others things will be added unto you.

I remember being devastated when a relationship that I was deeply involved in ended. I had no prayer life because I spent all of my time holding the phone talking to him—whomever *"the him"* was that month. I had no Word study time because I spent all of my time studying him, trying to get close to him and figured him out. I spent a majority of my time praising his achievements in an effort to move him when I should have been offering praise that moved God. I worshipped *"the him"* in my life because I exalted him to a place in my life above God. Wake up single woman! Wake up single man! Move that person out of God's seat. Idol worship is unacceptable! It is also a sin!

Some time ago I went to a football game in Atlanta. I noticed at a distance that some of the fans seemed to be having a problem with their seats. When the fans arrived at their seats to their surprise they found that there was another couple seated there. The people who were sitting in their seats acted like they did not want to move. But the discontented fans showed them their ticket stubs and went on to explain to them that they had paid for the seats that they had erred in occupying. They wanted the misplaced couple to hurry up and move so that they could sit down and enjoy the game.

For some of us that's just the way it is with our commitment to the Lord. Someone else or something is sitting in His seat! Jesus did not have to do it but He paid the price to sit in that place in your life. God sent His Son to die for our sins. Just like the couple presented their tickets, Jesus was crucified on the cross so that you could always see the record in the bible about how much He paid for His seat. The people did not want to move and neither will what's occupying the Lord's seat in your life. But it must move! The people wanted their tickets so that they could enjoy the game. God wants you to give Him His seat so that you can truly begin to enjoy the abundant life that He has planned just for you.

I remember once I heard a preacher diagnose many of the Christians in a waiting congregation as those suffering with a *"split personality"*. That is symptomatic of carnal Christians. We must refuse to be carnal Christians. We must not confess one thing with our mouth and then behave entirely different. Jesus must truly be the center of our joy. We cannot be true Christians and conform to the ways of the world. We must live seeking the Kingdom—God's way of doing things. That is the only way we will truly find rest and contentment.

Romans 14:17 For the kingdom of God is not meat or drink; but righteousness, and peace and joy in the Holy Ghost.

We waste God's valuable gift of time devoting ourselves to relationships that God has never ordained. Try being hopelessly devoted to the Lord. You will visit places in His glory that you never thought were possible. David the psalmist had a heart for God. He knew the blessedness of being devoted to the Lord!

Ps. 27:4 One thing have I desired of the Lord, that will I seek after; that I may dwell in the house of the Lord all the days of my life to behold the beauty of the Lord and to inquire in his temple.

You must arrive at the place of no compromise in your life where you want God above everything else. Everything means everything! We must die to self if we really want to live for Christ!

Luke 10:40-42 But Martha was distracted with all her preparations; and she came up to Him and said, "Lord, do you not care that my sister has left me to do all the serving alone, then tell her to help me." But the Lord answered and said to her, "Martha, Martha, you are worried and bothered about so many things; but only one thing is necessary, for Mary has chosen the good part, which shall not be taken away from her."

Mary made a decision to choose Jesus. Martha was busy in the kitchen doing things that were important but Mary chose the one thing that was necessary.

When we work on getting the **"one thing"** right everything else in our lives will fit right into place so that the well-planned celebration that God has for your life may begin. As a single person it's fine to have *"tunnel vision"* for Jesus.

When Isaac found Rebecca she was working tending her father's sheep. Focus on the present task wholeheartedly and Isaac will find you. Men don't look for a woman who is looking for a man. Look for a woman who is being faithful to the task at hand and seeking the face of *"The Man"*.

As a single person you do not have to confer with a spouses schedule before making a decision. Babysitters, and school schedules may not be your concern. As a single person you are free to serve with no restrictions.

I find great joy in being able to spend time with the Lord. If spending time with the Lord does not excite you then there needs to be some major adjustments in your thinking! I can seek the face of God anytime I want for as long as I want. God can use me for ministry at anytime because I am available!

Meditate on the words to this song.

Lord I'm available to you. My will I give to you. I do what you say to use me Lord to show someone the way and enable me to say. My storage is empty I am available to you.
(Word Records, 1995).

1.   Identify areas of your life that that hold the greatest commitment. Usually those areas are where we find the greatest security and pleasure. Do you think those areas of strong commitment please God? Why or Why not?

2.   So many of us obligate ourselves out of God's will. Make a list of responsibilities that you have assumed that are not yours.   Write down your plan to release yourself from those areas.

3.   Many believe that it is impossible for men and women to be involved in a strictly platonic relationship. Do you agree or disagree? Why?

4.   Have you violated boundaries in relationships in the past? How did that affect you and the person you were in relationship with? How were secondary people (children, parents, co-workers, etc.) in the relationship affected?

5.   Have you ever demanded the fulfillment of an I.O.U? How did that make you feel as a Christian? How do you think the person felt that received the request?

6.   As a single person we should never express eros love. Eros love is reserved for the marriage bed. How can you demonstrate phileo (friendly), and agape love (unconditional) with the people in your immediate surroundings?

7.   List some opportunities that you can take advantage of during this season of singleness for your life.

8.   Ps. 27 David desired one thing most of all in his life. How can you get closer to the Lord? What areas of your life must be submitted to God so that you can get to the *"One Thing"* in your life?

YOU ARE MY EVERYTHING

Jesus you are my everything
Nothing can fill the place in me that you made just for you
Nothing can be bought, borrowed or traded, no
Nothing will ever do

There is not enough comfort, understanding or love
What I need most cannot come from around me but comes only
from above
Your eyes have been attentively watching, waiting for my call
Waiting patiently for me to say that I surrender all

Now I know all that I have
And all that I am is because of you
Only you can guide me ever so true
Now I know how to respond I know what I must do

When loneliness quietly whispers I'll respond Jesus is my company
When the chains of despair try to hold me I'll respond Jesus is my
liberty

To depression I will boldly declare that Jesus is the lifter of my
head My sustainer and my peace
To temptation I proudly declare Jesus is my strength
I can glory even when I am weak

When hard questions probe my mind Jesus is my counselor, friend,
and confidant
In times of hurt and need of a helping hand
Jesus is my healer, my support, and my joy
I stand sure and firm because Jesus is the anchor of my soul, my
King, and my Lord,

Every supposed end springs forth new beginnings because He is my
resurrection, my way, my truth, and my life

The reason I inhale and exhale
The reason I hold fast to him as my stronghold
The reason I have faith to believe

 Simply put ….

JESUS IS MY EVERYTHING!

"Those Who

Love Best

Love First"

Learning To Love Others

These simple questions have answers that speak volumes about the way you love!

HONESTLY ANSWER TRUE OR FALSE

1. _____I expect to receive more love than I give.
2. _____I only love those who love me.
3. _____I only give love to those people that I know intimately.
4. _____I always love best when I am loved first.
5. _____People look to me to learn about God's love.
6. _____When I give love it will eventually be returned from that same person that the love was extended toward.
7. ____I yield myself daily to loving my fellow man.
8. _____People I am in relationship with must earn my love.
9. ____Love must always have conditions that protect those who are involved in the relationship.
10. _____ It is both possible and permissible to love God and not love my neighbor.
11. _____We must never make an effort to love. Love should just come naturally.
12. _____The relationships that I have with my family members are characterized by consistent godly expressions of love.
13. _____ I express the love of God very well in every area of my life.
14. _____ The "love walk" that I have with the Lord is a great foundation for building a marriage.

E Expects the best in every place

V Ventures to be manifested

O Overcomes every offense

L Lives To Love

1John 4:7 –8+11-13 Beloved, let us love one another, for love is from God; and everyone who loves is born of God and knows God. The one who does not love does not know God, for God is love. Beloved, if God so loved we also, ought to love one another. No one has seen God at any time; if we love one another, God abides in us, and His love is perfected in us. By this we know that we abide in Him and He in us because He has given us His Spirit.

Our season of singleness is an excellent time to allow God to develop us in our love walk. Love is the most important basic principal in living a victorious life in Jesus.

1Cor. 13 (Message Bible)
Love never gives up. Love cares more for others than for self. Love doesn't want what it does not have. Love doesn't strut; Doesn't have a swelled head; Doesn't force itself on others; Isn't always "me first," Doesn't fly of the handle; Doesn't keep score of the sins of others; Doesn't revel when others grovel; Takes pleasure in the flowering of truth; Puts up with anything; Trusts God always; Always looks for the best; Never looks back; But keeps going to the end.

We must love! If the pattern of our love is out of order we will never learn to love others. Following this pattern of love will mature us and bring us to higher dimensions in the Lord:

You will experience true joy by putting
*J*esus first
*O*thers second and
*Y*ourself last.
The basic concept of true love is **SACRIFICE!**

When we have begun to master some of the difficult lessons of love we will lovingly embrace the ones who are closest to us. That is not as easy as it sounds. The ones who are closets to us are usually the ones that we expect the most from. They are also usually the same ones that end up disappointing and hurting us the most.

Pro. 27:6 Faithful are the wounds of a friend; but the kisses of an enemy are deceitful.

In my own life I have found it easier to exercise deeds of love to those that I am not intimately related to. My family members and closest friends demand the greatest expressions of my love. We often think that it is a given for our brothers and sisters to give us the deepest and greatest expression of unconditional love. However, that is often not the case. The level of expectation for our family members love is so high that a family member's offense some how cuts much deeper than that of a person we are not related to.

Singles learn how to love by starting to love your family members. Love your alcoholic uncle. Love the stepbrothers and stepsisters that do not like you. Love your stepmother or your father who only calls on holidays and birthdays. Love the brother who beat you up as a child just because he could. Love the sister who never wanted to share or the cousin with the bad reputation. Believe it or not, loving like this is preparation for learning how to love your mate. True love always loves unconditionally.

1John 4:20 If someone says, "I love God," and hates his brother, he is a liar; for the one who does not love his brother whom he has seen, cannot love God whom he has not seen.

When you experience difficulty loving siblings or other family members whom you see on a regular basis how can you love your spouse whom you will see everyday rain or shine. Parents cannot un-son or un-daughter their children. As Christians we cannot divorce our parents regardless of what the world says! Your family will always be family just as your spouse is always meant to be your spouse. Never go into marriage considering the so-called *"easy option"* of divorce to remedy the disappointment of character flaws, inadequate cleaning or personal hygiene habits.

God gave you an imperfect family and He will give you a spouse with all of their quirks. Love them anyway. No one is perfect. Doesn't God love you! But God demonstrates His own love toward us, in that, while we were yet sinners, Christ died for us (Rom. 5:8). Could it be that God gave you that family to work a change in you so that God's love in you could change them? Isn't that something? Wow, God finds pleasure in using imperfect vessels to minister His perfect love.

John 3:16 For God so loved the world that He gave his only begotten Son that whosoever believeth in Him shall not perish but have everlasting life.

Love is not an option. Love is a must. Love is so powerful that it will help us to survive every disappointment and tragedy of life. If I remember correctly, and I know that I do, it was an act of love that set us free from the bondage of sin. It was an act of love that unlocked the chains that held us captive in lack and want. Love took the sting out of death and snatched victory from the grave. One an act of love has given us all everlasting life. Never underestimate the power of love!

For some of us our parents—our first teachers, did not show us real love. Others of us have been in a relationship that took much more than was ever given. Then still others of us have a definition of love that has been shaped by the distorted perspectives of the world. Therefore, a realistic understanding of love has never been established. I encourage you to make a decision to allow God to teach you of His love so that you can learn to love the way that Jesus loves. His love is liberating! When we fail to truly love we fail to truly live.

> **1John 4:19** We love because, he first loved us.

Those who love first love best. We often look for someone to love us before we love him or her, only in return. A true expression of love doesn't demand for someone to say I love you too. Relationships based on true love give others the *option* to accept and or return the love. We who are the body of Christ, desirous to be great lovers, and longing to be reduced to a beaming icon of love must go forth *initiating* the love of God. God loves best because He loved first. We love Him because He first loved us. As He constantly initiates His love for us we learn how to love others. When negative attitudes, opinionated mind-sets, suspicions, pessimisms and judgments are set aside we will all be reduced to nothing but love. We are to freely give love just because God freely gave it to us.

Luke 6:38 Give and it shall be given unto you good measure pressed down shaken together and running over shall men give into your bosom the same measure that you mete withal shall be measured unto you again.

When we give love, love will be returned to us. But, we set ourselves up for disappointment when we think that the love we express will automatically come back from the source that the love was extended toward. Watch out! The love will come from where you least expect it knocking you off your feet ministering to you when you need it most! At those times I am sure that you will be able to readily recognize that it is the Lord's doing and it will be marvelous in your eyes!

Eph. 5:1-2 (AMP) Therefore be imitators of God [copy Him and follow His example], as well-beloved children [imitate their father]. And walk in love, [esteeming and delighting in one another] as Christ loved us and gave Himself for us, a slain offering and a sacrifice, to God [for you, so that it became] a sweet fragrance

The more that we learn about the love of the Lord the easier it will be to relate and live productively as a single or married individual. Each of us must voluntarily surrender ourselves to God and ask Him to use us as vessels of His love. The bible tells us that we are all ambassadors for Christ (2Cor 5:20). We must look beyond ourselves, step outside our comfort zones and allow God to love through us. His love in us can change the corner of our world as we yield ourselves as living instruments that play melodious heart songs of His love.

 As a single person God wants you to enjoy your life to the fullest. Everyday He wants us to recognize that we have a reason to rejoice in Him. Pour into the lives of others. Die to your own desires and begin to live on the altar for God. Focus on living to bless the lives of others rather than sitting on the watchtower of your life looking for a blessing.

Pray this prayer:

Father, reveal to me every way that you love me so that I may be assured of your tender loving care and discover more reasons to praise you. Teach me to love others the way that you love me. Lord, I want the presence of your love to radiate from within me so that you may be glorified in every area of my life. In Jesus name Amen.

" My Friends Know How To Usher Me Into The Presence Of Jesus"

The Company That You Keep

Ps. 119:63 I am a companion of all them that fear thee, and of them that keep thy precepts
2 Cor. 6:14 AMP Do not be unequally yoked with unbelievers [do not make mismated alliances with them, or come under a different yoke with them, inconsistent with your faith]. For what partnership have right living and right standing with God with iniquity and lawlessness? Or how can light have fellowship with darkness?

As Christians we should always surround ourselves with Godly people. As single people of the kingdom of God it is important to ask God to lead you to single people who are progressively moving toward the Lord. Do not be deceived and misled! Evil companionship (communion, associations) corrupts and depraves good manners and morals and character (1 Cor. 15:33, AMP)

Mark 2:1-3 And when he had come back to Capernaum several days afterward, it was heard that He was at home. And many gathered together so that there was no longer room, not even near the door...And they came bringing to Him a paralytic, carried by four men.

These four men were all going in the same direction. They all had common goals and interests. The all wanted to get to Jesus. The four men, carried one man, who was lying on a bed inside to Jesus.

Football teams have better performance when there is an excited crowd of cheering fans. Studies show that people who exercise do a better job when they have a partner to workout with. People are generally the same even outside the realm of sports and exercise. It is always comforting to have someone to share your journey with who is striving toward having a closer relationship with the Lord and allowing the qualities of Jesus to be seen in their lives.

When you have found someone that you can openly and honestly share your struggles with and they are comfortable enough to share with you, it is priceless! Then you can glean richly from each other's experiences. When we learn from the mistakes or achievements of our friends experience does not have to be our best teacher.

Your inner circle should serve as your support base. If your inner circle is not supportive you need to quickly hokey pokey to another circle. Christians who are strong in the faith will help to keep you accountable. A friend loves at all times. If you are really going to be a friend you will always speak the truth in love even when it hurts. Real friends will always make you better. We need people around us that we can trust.

Pro. 27:1 (KJV) Iron sharpens iron; so a man sharpeneth the countenance his friend.
Pro. 11:14 Where no counsel is the people fall: but in the multitude of counselors there is safety.
Pro. 27:6 (NIV) Wounds from a friend can be trusted but an enemy multiplies kisses

When the men could not come through the press (crowd) they went through the roof. The trials and obstacles represented in the natural did not deter their quest to get to Jesus. We must have people around us that understand what it means to be called out from the world and sold out to God. We must have people around us who are not willing to compromise their Christian morals and beliefs.

Some of us give into sinful temptations that challenge our morality when it's a group effort.

Well, that's our friend, whom we have known since grade school. Let's go to the bachelor party together! We are not married, what difference does it make. Let's go to the bacheloret party. There won't be but one stripper! We are single! One drink won't hurt anything. Come on and take a hit. God gave it to us to enjoy together that's why it grows naturally.

Being single gives us freedom but not freedom to live a life free from God. We must never make the mistake of confusing our freedom with what is actually bondage to the power of sin.

The four men carried their friend on the bed because he had a problem. When your faith walk as a single person becomes weak your "company" ought to be able to carry you to the Lord. The faith of your companions ought to impact the weakness of your present situation so that your dead places come alive by the strength of their faith.

The company that you keep ought to lead you to the secret place in God so that you can hear a word from Him and receive exactly what you need. The four men kicked in the roof until they were standing in the room with their friend. Jesus responded to the faith of the four men, but he spoke to the man with palsy. Jesus said, "Son, thy sins be forgiven the."

When we are dealing with situations of life that have us paralyzed the faith of the company that we keep ought to lift us to where you need to be to get what we need from God.

THE COMPANY OF MY MARRIED FRIENDS
Lets, go a bit further to talk about the company that we keep. The desires of married people are much different than that of single people. As Christians you both love the Lord but a married person has different priorities. I am not saying that it is impossible for a married person and a single person to have a meaningful relationship but what I am saying is that you must be aware of the boundaries.

Proceed with caution! Single people can have married people

thinking about divorce and married couples will have single people jumping the broom. The enemy finds pleasure in using relationships between married and single people to stir up strife, jealousy and animosity. For some reason single people long to be attached to some one when they see their happily married friends together and when there is trouble in the marriage the presence of the free life of a single person can tempt a married person to walk right out the door!

It is fine to have friends who are married or single. Just be careful. You cannot always discuss everything. Neither can you pattern your single life after their married lives. Singles that spend too much time with married couples often feel like a third wheel and are regularly matched up in an attempt to fit in with their coupled friends.

Spend some time thinking about the people that you endearingly call friend then answer the following questions.

1.   What common godly interest and strengths do you share?

2.   Are there people around you that need to become an acquaintance rather than being your friend?

3.   How often do you and your friends pray together and discuss the scriptures?

4.   In times that you need spiritual guidance would you turn to any of the people in your inner circle knowing that you would receive what you need?

5. Do you do a better job keeping your friend in line or are you part of the reason that your friend is out of line?

6.   Can you be completely honest with your friends? If not, is that really your friend? Do you attack or appreciate your friends when they give you sound advice?

7.   In what ways have your friends become better because they are in relationship with you? In what way have you become better because your friends are a part of your life?

8.   Are most of your friends married or single? How do you respect and or overstep personal boundaries in those relationships?

The PRE-TEST

Honestly answer the following questions with the word always, sometimes, or never. Then read the following chapters. Answering these questions with a group makes for excellent constructive conversation.

1. I am _____ upfront about what I expect in my dating relationships.
2. When I date I _____ set relationships boundaries or express goals in fear of running the one whom I am dating away.
3. I _____ present the real me from the beginning of my dating relationships.
4. On first dates I _____ think that it is important to dress and behave in a way that is becoming to my date.
5. I _____ feel best when I transform to become my dates answer to his or her dream.
6. Sexual chemistry is _____ a good foundation for a great friendship.
7. A long term dating relationship _____ permits a sexual relationship.
8. My dates are _____ considered my brother or sisters in the Lord.
9. I _____ date in groups.
10. When I date I _____ feel pressured to be romantic.
11. There is _____ anything wrong with kissing on the first date or any date.
12. I _____ enjoy being alone with my date.
13. It is _____ impossible to be a friend and be romantically interested in the person that I date.
14. Career choice _____ makes a marked difference in choosing the person that I date.
15. Church attendance _____ makes a marked difference in choosing the person I date.
16. Whether a person has been married or not _____ affects whether I chose to date them.

17.   I _____ date people who are parents.
18.   The dating relationship is _____ a good indicator about what kind of marriage I would have with that person.
19.   Dating boundaries should _____ just apply to people who have never been married.
20.   Dating _____ affects my godly purpose and my future.
21.   Dating is _____ something that divorced, widowed or people over forty-five ever really do.
22.   My date should _____ pay my way.
23.   Going "dutch" on a date is _____ acceptable.
24.   When I pay for a date the one I pay for should _____ owe me something in return.
25.   When I date I _____ quickly fall head over heels in love.
26.   I have _____ mistaken lust or infatuation for love.
27.   My dating relationships _____ start off hot and end up cold.
28.   I am a woman but I think it is _____ unnecessary for my date to open my door and pull out my chair.
29.   My first date conversation is _____ about my previous relationships.
30.   My early dating relationships are _____ characterized by lengthy conversations and frequent visits.
31.   Kissing is _____ acceptable while dating.
32.   A great kiss is _____ a sign of the chemistry that makes for a great relationship.
33.   A spiritual connection is _____ more important than physical chemistry.
34.   Mature single Christians should _____ practice abstinence.
35.   Physical appeal is _____ priority when I date.
36.   I should _____ date as many people as I can while I am single.
37.   My body is _____ regarded as my own property.
38.   Fondling while dating is _____ acceptable.
39.   Oral sex is _____ permissible while dating.

40. Oral sex should_____ appear in the same category as sexual intercourse.
41. Anal sex is _____ classified as real sex.
42. Sexual relations_____ means sexual intercourse.
43. Sex while dating _____ depends on the person who you are dating.
44. I should _____ tell a person I am dating when my feelings change from friendly love to romantic love.
45. Topics like marriage, and family planning are _____ great topics of conversation while dating my friend.
46. I _____ set appearance criteria for my dates that determine the opportunity for future dates.
47. My dates must _____ be just as attractive as I am.
48. I am _____ happiest when my dating schedule is busy.
49. I _____ go out alone.
50. I _____ wait to go out with someone else.
51. My social life is _____ out of balance if I do not date regularly.
52. I have _____ missed opportunities because I waited or refused to go without an escort.
53. Sexual intercourse _____ fills a void in my life.
51. Masturbation is _____ acceptable.
52. Being a lesbian or homosexual is _____ an acceptable lifestyle.
53. I _____ struggle with loneliness as a single person.
54. I _____ think that when people are not married or with children by a certain age they ought to forget about it.
55. Single men should _____ be permitted to be more sexually active than women.
56. Meeting my date's family is _____ a good thing.
57. I _____ fear getting married.

"Wherever There Is Wordly Pressure Apply Godly Contentment"

DEALING WITH P-R-E-S-S-U-R-E

Pro. 3:5-6 Lean on, trust in, and be confident in the Lord with all your heart and mind and do not rely on your own insight or understanding. In all your ways know, recognize and acknowledge Him and He will direct and make straight and plain your paths.

The world places a lot of pressure upon singles to perform so that *"carnal expectations"* are meet. For that reason many singles spend an unprecedented amount of their time and energy attempting to successfully complete the objectives listed on the world's report card.

Consequently, many Christian singles label themselves as failures when particular standards are not met at just the right time.

Pro. 16:9 The mind of a man plans his way, but the Lord directs his steps.
Pro. 14: 12 There is a way that seems right to man but its end is the way of death.

When we really trust God we do not bend or break because of worldly pressures, neither do we feel the overwhelming desire to rush God, as if such a thing were possible. Any and everything that God has ordained to take place will happen in *"His timing"*.

We must remember that our lives are not to be shaped by the dictates of ungodly opinions and forced ambitions. When we follow the steps that have been ordered by God our vision will be God's vision, our desire will be God's desire and our predestined purpose will be brought to fruition.

Our purpose will be divinely decorated with whatever God deems necessary to bring it to completion. If a husband or wife is part of the plan we will have that person in our lives. If children are part of the plan then we will have children as well! We must all accept God's will for our lives because He knows best exactly what we need.

1 Tim 6:8 Godliness with contentment is great gain.

The wonderful weight of contentment and peace will apply incomprehensible pressure on the ungodly pressure that is coming against you—tempting you to compromise. Fulfilling the details of the worlds plan for our lives will disappointment God. But, when we satisfy the details of God's plan for our lives we will fill His heart with proud joy!

What I feared has come upon me; what I dreaded has happened to me. I have no peace, no quietness; I have no rest, but only turmoil **(Job 3:32,NIV).**

THE TICKING BIOLOGICAL CLOCK
Many single people want to have children early because they fear being too old to care for their children and vibrantly nurture their growth. They do not want to be mistaken for their own child's grandparents. Men want to be able to painlessly toss the football around and women feel like their biological clock is going to wind down before they are able to deliver a healthy and happy baby.

In today's society it is a popular thing for women and men to become involved in ungodly relationships so that they may conceive. Learn from the example of Sarah, taking matters into your own hands can birth an Ishmael to deal with and make matters much worse (Gen. 16). Never put the cart before the horse. That's a good way to go nowhere fast. As believer's we must learn to pray that God's will be done in our lives and allow Him to lead us by His spirit.

Some of the best parental figures never birth their own

children. It may not be God's plan for you to bare or conceive children. Maybe God wants you to give a child a chance at life through adoption or foster parenting. Some of the best parental role models are simply loving and responsible adults.

TOO OLD FOR THE HONEY MOON

You are never too old to marry. Sometimes we are not married yet because we have not completed our season of preparation for our mate. The preparation needed for marriage is based on the individual. I know in my own life God was doing a lot of men a favor by keeping them away from me. I would have run a husband away. Not to mention all the brokenness in my life that needed to be healed before I could commit to anyone. I believe that God has prepared me to be a blessing for marriage. If I had married in my time I would have been more of a burden.

Remember, you are never too old to marry! Some people are ready at twenty-five, thirty and still others are not ready until sixty-five or even older. Do not doubt God. Believe me He does know what He is doing. At just the right moment in time God will wake up your Adam or present your Eve. When God brings your groom or your bride you will be glad that you waited.

S.S 2:7 Do not arouse or awaken love until it so desires

DO NOT BE FOOLED BY THE WORLD

Lev. 18:22 You shall not lie with a male as one lies with a female, it is abomination (disgust)
Lev. 20:13 If there is a man who lies with a male, as those who lie with a woman, both of them have committed a detestable act...

Being single does not give you permission to experiment with or willfully live alternative lifestyles. Life partners—homosexual and lesbian relationships are not acceptable in the sight of God. Who cares what the world says. The world's wisdom is not the authority. God's word is the only and final authority. I believe the word of God. Do you? Popular demand may sway the standards of the world but it will never change God's standard for holiness. God made the woman for the man; God did not make the woman for the woman or the man for the man. Do not be fooled by the façade of your pain. For some turning toward the same sex may appear to cure loneliness and bring comfort and acceptance but I insist, take a moment and honestly look within. I can gurantee that you will discover that the root of your desire is planted in circumstances much deeper than loneliness or unbridled passion.

THE BURNING DESIRE
Submit yourself to God **THEN** (emphasis added) Resist the devil and he will flee **(James 4:7)**

What do you do when your hormones are raging? Whenever a single person is involved in sexual relationship outside marriage they are breaking covenant with God. If you cannot be true to your commitment outside of marriage to God it's called fornication but in the bonds of marriage it's called adultery. Marriage will not halt sexual promiscuity. If you do not have self-control outside of marriage you will not have it within the bonds of matrimony either.

Sexual desires are normal but they *can be* controlled and managed. As Christians we can exercise self-control. Submit this area unto God first, then when you resist the devil he will flee. I know that I can do all things through Christ who strengthens me (Phil. 4:13). How about you? The important question is, do you want to overcome?

SEX IS FOR TWO ONLY NOT ONE

1Peter 2:11,(Amp) Beloved, I implore you as aliens and strangers and exiles [in this world] to abstain from sensual urges (evil desires, the passions of the flesh, your lower nature) that wage war against the soul.

Masturbation is not the answer to satisfying sexual desire. Masturbation is only a pursuit to fulfill lust. Lust is an intense craving; *not always sexual*. It is an overwhelming desire, eagerness or enthusiasm. Lust *has the power* to become obsessive (American Heritage Dictionary,1995). Lust is always hungry for more and deceptively promises more power and satisfaction.

Masturbation opens the door for sexual self-gratification. It may begin with fondling but there is often a tendency to move on to things like pornography and the use of other "*devices*" that openly welcome more sinful behavior. These behaviors can become addictive and develop an increasing longing for more just like a drug. A life of lust can potentially lead to homosexuality, prostitution, and other perverse behaviors.

Men of lust often have difficulty understanding intimacy in marriage relationships because rewarding lustful appetites with habitual lustful behavior is approved by the world as an acceptable way of life for the single man. When a lustful man marries he does not understand that the same behavior that satisfied the lustful women will not work with his wife who needs more than just physical affection. A man of lust only knows how to have sex. He does not know how to make love.

Women define a good marriage as one marked with intimacy and romance. *It's not just* the act of sexual intercourse that brings her pleasure. Making love is more mental for women than it is physical for men and the process of making love for both must being long before they enter the bedroom.

Single women who masturbate will discover emotional intimacy with others that will stimulate them while loosing desire for a husband to be because she has learned to please herself all by herself hence, lessening the desire for a healthy sexual relationship within a marriage. Deriving emotional intimacy from other sources and providing her own sexual pleasure may eventually cause a woman to lose desire for a male companion completely.

NOT ALONE AND NOT LONELY
Matt. 28: 20b I am with you always...

In this life we must recognize that as children of God we are NEVER alone. God said that He would never leave us nor for-sake us. When we acknowledge the presence of our Lord we tap into his abiding companionship, and comfort. We come to know Him as our friend.

As a member of the body of Christ we always have brothers and sisters that we can enjoy by sharing and encouraging one another in the love of Lord. A man that hath friends must show himself friendly (Pro. 18:24).

God always provides what we need when we ask. Ask God to give you Godly companions according to His word. One day God showed me how He has always made sure that I felt His love. It was in families. Families are just extensions of God's love. I am single and an only child. Throughout my life God has given me several large families to unite with as an expression of His love. God sets the lonely in families (Ps 68: 6, NIV). As children of The Lord we never have to be lonely and we are never alone.

1.   What truths has God just revealed to you that will

eliminate and or adjust the strength of the pressures in your life as a single Christian?

2.   Sometimes the result of yielding to the pressures of our flesh and our peers results in sin. What sin do you need to confess to God?

3.   The enemy's traps are subtly set. Many times we do not notice his trap until we get caught. The bible says give no place to the devil (Eph 4:27). Think about **"the pressures"** that you feel in your single life. How has the devil subtly set traps and what place have you given him in your life?

4.   Have you ever gotten ahead of God? What happened when you tried to make things happen rather than waiting on God?

5.   In your own words write down what it means to trust God.

Kiss Me Not

Kiss me
No Kiss Me Not
Kiss Me
No
Kiss Me Not

Well, if you truly love me you can kiss me
I'm glad to hear your love is true
Go ahead and kiss me then, a lot but not right there!
Not until I say I do

Kiss me
No
Kiss Me not
Kiss Me
No
Kiss Me Not

Since our first kiss things have really changed
Will I see you again tonight?
You stay on your side and I'll sleep on mine
It's okay
I'm sure
Everything is all right

Kiss me
No, Kiss me not
Kiss Me
No
Kiss Me Not

I agree you go your way and I'll go mine
Why can't I let go of what I thought I left behind?
Don't leave me!
Now whom do you love ever so true?

Connection accomplished
Deposit now made
Each relation from this point on is but a masquerade
Kiss me! No! KISS Me NOT!

To Date AND Whom Not To Date? That's The Question!!!

THE DOs AND DON'Ts OF DATING

DO:

1. State your expectations in the beginning.

Problems are inevitable within a relationship when each person begins with a completely different end in mind. Clearly stating your individual expectations on the front end saves both time and energy. Being honest about your individual expectations will allow each person in a dating relationship to be respectful of boundaries, relax and dispel any hidden desires.

2. Be yourself

I have listened to countless testimonies from people who date one person and then suddenly find that they have married someone totally different. One day they suddenly discover that they have been living with a stranger and sleeping with the enemy. Couples involved in a prolonged courtship usually share the same testimony. When we meet new people we always want to put our best foot forward and that is okay because first impressions are very important, but the "foot" that is put forward must be the foot that you are willing to put forward throughout the relationship. Never start what you cannot continue doing wholeheartedly.

Deceptive dating tactics of flattery lure people to fall in love with a façade. Dating should not be a performance that demonstrates how well you can portray the person that you wish you were or the person your date wants you to be. The stress, strain and headache of "trying to impress", is not worth it. When your date would rather have the person that you create they are not really interested in you.

3. Seek to build a friendship

I remember watching those "dating shows" on television as a teenager. The bottom line of the entire match-make was to find out if the couple had chemistry. The couple that had the *"the strongest chemical reaction"*, or so to speak was considered to have the best time on their date compared to those couples who just enjoyed each others company and had great conversation.

Those dating shows used a primetime platform to glorify fornication and carnal perspectives of sexuality. A strong desire to be intimately involved prompted many of the featured singles to put the cart before the horse.

Dating should not be considered an excuse to be promiscuous. Dating should be considered an official time set aside to become more acquainted with someone. Building a friendship means spending sharing time together. It means getting to know your brother or sister in Christ. Remember, if you would not do it with your sister or brother, YOU SHOULD NOT BE DOING IT!

4. Date in groups

Dating in groups helps to build camaraderie. The group dating style also helps you get to know more of the specifics about the person you are interested in. Dating in groups gives you an opportunity to observe how your date interacts with other people. Dating one on one may give a biased perspec-tive.

Dating in groups also helps to lessen the pressure of being *"romantic"*. The presence of others around keeps both parties within set boundaries and reinforces accountability.

5. Be selective about who you date

You do not have to go out with everyone that asks! You have the right to pick and choose. Desperation should never be your motivation for going out! Ask Jesus He is your Lord. Would He be pleased with the person we are thinking about going out with?

Use your time wisely. There are some people that we just spend time with and there are other people who we invest time in. Then there are those whom we do not consider at all. Your time is valuable! Your spirit is very sensitive. Don't allow just anybody to speak into your life. Our personal life today is the result of every good, bad and indifferent experience we had on our yesterdays. Date with purpose and destiny in mind. Date people who are going to help you move forward. Don't spend time with people who will impede or retard your progress.

6. Be prepared to pay your own way

People often get the wrong idea and make assumptions when it comes to paying for a date. If one person pays for the other it must be simply because they desire to be a blessing, period. Never think that money spent on a date accrues a debt payable on demand. Some big spenders claim that the more expensive a date the greater the debt. For instance, dinner may be worth a hug and a kiss. Dinner, a movie and flowers may be worth a hug and a "*good*" kiss or a sleep over depending on the easiness of the escorted. Whatever! I do not think so! Sounds like prostitution to me. Go "dutch"! Paying your own way keeps things simple and eliminates the possibility of insincere acts of kindness.

7. Move Slowly

Whenever we date someone new it can be very exciting, especially if we have not dated in a while and the person really appeals to us. But, be very careful moving into a relationship too fast may cause us to confuse emotion, hope, and lust with real love and intimacy that could lead to impermissible sex.

8. Meet the family

I have discovered if a man truly loves and respects his mother he has a greater tendency to have that same attitude towards the woman he dates. In the same way a woman who has a loving relationship with her father is also likely to express the same honorable attitude toward the man she dates. Your date is a representative of their entire family saga including every success, failure and generational curse- mental, physical, social, and economical. Make a point to spend time with your friend's family members. You will gain foresight about the quality of the relationship your friend may have with you.

DON'T:

1. Spill your guts on the first date

James 1:19 ...be swift to hear, slow to speak...

Your first date should not be a counseling session to help you with your prior relationship. No one wants to hear your sob story on the first date. I have heard it time a time again. " He was there for me when we broke up and one thing led to another.

In those instances a real relationship has been confused with someone that got caught on the rebound because they were broken up because of the break up! Never confuse moments of consolation with intriguing conversation just because you may have matched old wounds.

Everyone you date should not become your dumping ground! Choose your words carefully. Be very wise about what you say, when you say it and how you say it!

2. Kiss and Touch

Keep your hands to yourself. I know what you are thinking. Well, if we just kiss there is nothing wrong with that, right? Keep your tongue in your mouth and your saliva to yourself! Some say, "Well, if we kiss I can tell if there is anything there—you know, if we have chemistry. Well, let me tell you something, if you find the person attractive, I can gurantee that there will be chemistry. In other words your *flesh* will react! You know what you are thinking when you are kissing and touching! There is no sense in waking up the flesh! Let sleeping dogs lie! As single saints we must mature in the Lord to the point that we are not just concerned with making our liver quiver! Wouldn't you rather have a connection with someone who makes your spirit leap?

It all starts with a kiss! A kiss opens the door and fondling says you're welcome come on in! Now I will admit I have not always felt this way but the closer I get to the Lord the more I realize that it is my responsibility to guard my temple. My temple is like a church building and the Holy Ghost dwells in me. As a Christian I respect the sanctuary of God. If I am being asked to do something I would not do in the sanctuary of God I do not do it.

3. Spend too much time together

Sending too much time together forces premature commitment. When we are dating we should spend time not with a sense of urgency but with prudent discretion. Spending all of your time "holding the phone," talking into the wee hours of the night is a mistake. Even though you may want to spend more time together in the beginning do the smart thing. Allow sufficient time to pass between your dates. Remember, you are dating. You are not married! Being conservative with your time will cause you to look forward to the next time that you are together. Too much time spent together could be an over kill. Everyone needs room to breath. I believe I heard someone say once that absence makes the heart grow fonder!

4. Immediately take your dates on the marriage tract

Do not impose upon your dates. It is important not to immediately label them as Mr. or Mrs. Right. When this behavior is evident it is obvious that the person is so in love with the idea of marriage that anyone will do. Guess what? They have chosen you!

Discussing marriage, naming the kids, and planning the purchase of a home and the family car are not the greatest topics of discussion for a dating couple unless the relationship has changed its goal.

A dating couple is different from a couple that is engaged to be married. When a couple is dating and the male intends to ask for the female's hand in marriage those things are acceptable for discussion but "***the other do's and don'ts still apply***". Those involved in a relationship should make it known when their feelings change from friendly love to romantic love. Now that personal objectives have changed new boundaries and expectations may need to be established.

5. Dating Around

Smokey Robinson's mamma may not have given him the best

advice when she told him that, "he better shop around!" Every time we engage in a serious relationship for an extended period of time we open ourselves up emotionally making soul ties that are not easily unloosed.

When I was in high school I never thought that dating a guy for a long time was a bad thing. Actually, I thought that it was the better thing to do. The mistake I made was that I treated every relationship as if it was meant to " last forever". As a result I was usually devastated when the relationship ended. I dated unwisely and set both unattainable and unrealistic goals for the relationship. When the reality of the circumstances (age, maturity, and future aspirations) stood boldly before me my hopes crumbled into pieces. Too much of my life was wastefully sacrificed and sadly missed.

6. Overestimating Yourself

Do you remember the story of David in the bible? He was anointed to be king when he was a boy (1Sam 16:7+12). Neither his brothers nor his father thought he was king material but God new differently. Samuel, the prophet, was sent to anoint David as the new king. But, like many of us Samuel got caught up in outer appearance and stature. He thought that David's brother Eliab or one of the other brothers should be king because they "looked the part".

God had to open Samuel's eyes with understanding so that he could see that it is not the outer appearance that we should be concerned about, but it is the heart. That which is firm will eventually be loose; that which is lifted will eventually drop; and that which is flat will eventually bulge and shake (Ps. 451?). Never think so highly of yourselves that you miss the blessing that God has for you. Don't miss your king or queen because they do not complete your physique "checklist". Your interest ought to go past the surface. Besides, God knows exactly what mate best complements your God given purpose. God is not making you hold out for an "Elmer

Fudd" or "Ragedy Ann". If God has a mate for you he or she will be beautiful in your eyes. Anyway, when did you become perfect!!!

7. Dating Schedule

Dating should fit into your schedule you should not live to make your schedule around your dating. If you want to go somewhere just go! If you want to do something just do it! You will starve to death waiting for someone to take you to dinner. That movie you want to see will not always be showing. See the movie before it goes to the archives!

Life is filled with opportunities don't miss out on life because you are waiting on an escort. Who knows whom you may meet once you get there! Our dating lives or the lack there of should not dictate our social lives. We can still be sociable, well balanced people without a full dating schedule.

My History, My Hope, My Healing

A testimony I remember so vividly
About a sweet young lady's virginity

Her other soul knew her quite so well
Any hidden secrets were not necessary to tell
The spirit revealed to her He knew each secret you see
About every hidden dark sullen well kept m-y-s-t-e-r-y

For her other soul knew without her even making a peep
Her other soul knew what ever would she do

At their next time of leisure
As they were making their change
The sweetness did hide herself in undying shame

Her nakedness once beauty now must be covered when bare
The innocence was gone
Only God could repair

The sincerity of their testimony I now comprehend
The same brand of deception became my close and dear friend
I both welcomed and shunned filth so clean soon became sin

Inevitably shame did willfully arise
I with regret do sadly surmise
Embarrassment's had its face turned high not turned down low
Defining the many dreary places my spirit did reluctantly go

I no longer saw myself with the purity I once knew
All my skies grew even darker, once gray never blue
Unable to catch the beauty of even others in view
The reality became buried
Did I even recognize what was once so joyously true

Nakedness God's masterpiece
Now recalled but driven images and surfaced the result of sins savage beast

All my innocence was now forgotten pushed under the rug
As was then until most recently I went looking for real love

Stand before me boldly and your presence will allow me to see
You have the key to help me overcome my dark well-kept mystery
To adore the beauty of God's wonderful gift again
Painfully healing deeply beginning to sift

Sifting away the learned behavior I dreaded to share
Just assure me that you will be there to tell me that it's okay
As I submit my other soul wash the dirty images away

After all the wrong
I am tired of singing this depressed and awful song

Turning my head and closing my eyes
I will not look nor will I speak
The place of peace is what I desperately seek

No more a source of pain
Smiles changed from a frown
You lifted up my head from casting shame to the ground

My surrender has lifted the burden I feel
A vessel of God's understanding
I am beginning to heal

SEX!

#6 "DO YOU HAVE IT ???"

Lets Talk About Sex

Let's talk about sex! What is sex? I want to be sure that we are reading from the same page—gender is not what I am referring to here. I am talking about sexual intercourse-- *sexual relations*. The reason that so many of us are in such bad shape is because no one ever appropriately talked to us about sex.

Sex is a normal part of life. Sex is not nasty. Sex is the reason that you exist. However, it is off limits to YOU as a single person. Sex is a love expression *reserved* for a husband and his wife. Please notice that I did not say that sex was reserved for a man and a woman. Sex is reserved for a husband and *his* wife.

I want to make it as plain as possible so that there is no mistake. Sexual intercourse is not a permissible act for a single person . If you are engaged to be married—you still are not married so there should still be no sex. If you have been dating for years—you are still not married so —no sex. If you are living together you are still not married and you are living in sin so—sorry still no sex. I know what you are thinking. What if we used to be married and we are thinking about getting back together? Thinking about reuniting and being married are two entirely different situations—sorry still no sex! What if we are in love? Nope, sorry still no sex. If you really love each other then you both want what's best for each other and going against God's order is not what is best. The bed of fornication is defiled and is disgust in the sight of God.

I recently, heard testimonies from Christian couples that think oral sex is permissible because it is not the same as sexual intercourse and allows an individual to maintain their virgin status. The devil is a liar. Don't let him fool you!   The word virgin does not only define a person who has not had sexual intercourse. The word virgin also means, untouched, unused or pure (Webster's, 1995). Oral sex does not leave one pure. As a matter of fact a person can contract just as many STD's by mouth as by sexual intercourse. Oral sex and every variation of premarital sex deeply affect our individual personality, character and spiritual intellect. Sex includes all and any sexual relations. According to The Heritage dictionary sex is the sexual urge or instinct as it manifests itself in behavior. So, if the sexual urge manifest as anal sex, oral sex, group sex, sexual intercourse, fondling, or petting, sex is still sex. Therefore, if you are a single person all of the aforementioned is absolutely forbidden.

1Cor. 6:18-19 Shun immortality and all sexual looseness [flee from impurity in thought, word or deed]. Any other sin which a man commits is one outside the body. But he commits sexual immorality sins against his own body(Amp).

God's word is not written to restrict us from pleasure but to protect us from causing damage to our lives. When an individual becomes involved in a sexual relationship he or she opens themselves up to a world of feelings, responsibilities and emotions that they have never experienced. Sexual intercourse opens up a place within us for intimacy on a different level. Once that door has been opened that place of intimacy in us will always long to be filled. When it is not filled the individual may experience loneliness and depression that lead to feelings of incompleteness.

1Cor. 7:1b-2 It is good for a man not to touch a woman. Nevertheless, because of temptation to impurity and to avoid immorality, let every man have his own wife, and let every woman have her own husband (Amp).

People who are sexually active come to know something about themselves and their partners that they never knew before. In the bible the word that is often used to describe sexual intimacy is "know" or the past tense of the word, "knew". For example in Gen 4:1 Adam knew Eve his wife and she conceived and bare Cain. When we are sexually intimate we disclose privileged, confidential knowledge about ourselves. Sexual intimacy welcomes both an exchange and a connection.

During sexual intercourse there is an exchange of blood that binds the blood covenant that should only be bound between a husband and wife. Consummation, the blood covenant, by way of sexual intercourse, is what completes the wedding ceremony. Therefore, in a *sense* we are married to everyone that we ever had sexual intercourse with. Even further we bring all those people to bed with us when we do finally sleep with our husband or wife. Thank God for the blood of Jesus. If we confess our sins, He is faithful and righteous to forgive us our sins and cleanse us from all unrighteousness **1 John 1:9.**

Gen 2:24 Therefore, shall a man leave his father and mother, and be joined to his wife; they shall become one flesh.

The gift of virginity can only be given away one time. The precious gift is only to be given to your husband or wife. People are much more happy about receiving a gift that has never been opened rather than receiving a gift that others have seen and handled. Don't shop around. No one really wants *"experienced merchandise"*. A godly mate will be honored to know that you protected and saved their gift.

Some say that I need to be experienced sexually before I get married so that I can please my mate and sexual experience helps me know what to look for in a future mate. When there is no one to compare with your mate will *"automatically"* please you. Experience only makes it more difficult for your future mate to please you if they are forced to compete with all of your *"experience"*. God created the bodies of both men and women to adjust to their partners sexually. Don't worry. A union that is made and blessed by God gives opportunity for a highly enjoyable sexual experience.

I know that living single and dealing with natural sexual desire is not always easy. For some of us, our lifestyles have become accustomed to always having someone around. What do you do when you are not a virgin anymore but now you know better? What do you do with desire that has been awakened leaving you hungry for more? I look at it like this. I never knew that French Vanilla ice cream was good until I tasted it. Now I know it's good because I have tasted it. As a matter of fact it is so good to me that I crave it from time to time. If I never tasted it, I would never crave it. But I cannot have the ice cream every time I want it because eating it whenever I want to is not always good for me. The same principles must be applied to our sex lives.

Having sex as a single person opened the door to desires that should have never been welcomed into our lives. That does not mean that your body does not still desire a sexual relationship. But, what that does mean is now you know what is best for you and even though your body craves sex you must listen to your spirit when it says no! Dealing with those feelings is the consequence you have to live with for making a choice outside of God's will.

1Cor 10:13 No temptation has overtaken you but such as is common to man; and God is faithful, who will not allow you to be tempted beyond what you are able, but with the temptation will provide the way of escape also, so that you will be able to endure it.

If you are divorced or widowed regardless of the language your body is talking your spirit still must say no! However, if you would like to be married again ask God to send you a mate. As Paul says it is better to marry than to burn (1Cor 7:9).

But in the meantime the same thing still applies to you too—
NO SEX!

Be honest with yourself about sexual triggers. Many of us
easily fall into the traps of the devil because we will not be
honest with ourselves about our weaknesses. So the devil gets
us every time. Stop walking around in denial! The devil knows
just what kind of *"cheese to put on our trap"* and many of us
take the bait each time he sets the trap.

Do not make a habit of feeding your flesh things that will stir
up your sexual emotions. Stop rehashing old love affairs,
reading old cards and looking at old pictures. That behavior
can start something you'd wish later you had never begun.
Watching movies and soap operas filled with *"flesh"*, or reading
smut novels and listening to songs with explicit lyrics can
really mess you up. We are whatever we eat?

Pro. 4:23-26(Amp) Keep and guard your heart with all viligance and
above all that you guard, for out of it flow the springs of life. Put
away from you false and dishonest speech, and willful contrary talk
put far from you. Let your eyes look right on [with fixed purpose],
and let your gaze be straight before you. Consider well the path of
your feet, and let all your ways be established and ordered a right.

Images that we think that we see for only a moment register
in our subconscious mind and play coming attractions at the
immediate demand of our flesh. The more exposed our minds
are toward worldly pictures of joy and pleasure (pseudo love)
the easier it is for our minds to create ungodly images that
increase the enemy's arsenal of ammunition to war against us.

The Abduction of Innocence
Images etched in innocence
Easily discovered yet difficult to erase
Shaping my expectation
Guiding me away from God's presence
Subtly luring me toward disgrace

Appealing and pleasurable a top the pedestal of the world's wisdom
Popular among the kindred deceived
Walking with blinders on
Desperately longing for empty dreams
Constant intense demonstrations surround me
Demanding compliance or so it seemed

Tainted, spoiled, terribly discontent
Driven toward unfulfilling desires
God never intended nor ever meant

A convenient exchange
God's will for their carnal ambitions
Designed to wickedly nourish my deep-rooted inhibitions

Carbon copies of deception
A realistic illusion to a green mind
A perplexing dilemma
Welcomed by repeating encounters of the worst kind

Revelation now fuses the light that shines
A trampled heart
A broken spirit
Distortions and delusions of my mind

Never knew the glorious road
Holiness, Righteousness, Purity, ancient fiction never told
Sacred experiences polluted
Surviving the damage but now
The real truth slowly unfolds

Heartfelt repentance yields restoration and revival of the dead
Salvages and seals the remnants of my soul
Owner of words that rescue
No longer mine to hold

Responding to the ransom note
The priceless gift prepaid
Betrothed to the savior soon coming
With earnest expectation
I am pleased and patiently waiting!

My Pledge
of
Chastity

Father, I vow not to be sexually involved with anyone

until I am married to the mate that you have chosen for me.

I understand that my virginity is a wonderful gift to be given only to my

husband or wife.   I know that with The Christ I can triumph over every temptation.

I choose to live a chaste life because I know that is your will .

My desire is for you to be glorified in me.

In Jesus Name

Amen.

_____   _____
(First and Last name)   (Date)

My Pledge
of
Chastity

Father, I vow not to be sexually involved with anyone until I am married to the mate that you have chosen for me. I confess my sin of sexual immorality and I receive your forgiveness and my cleansing according to 1John 1:9. I now rededicate my entire body to you. I am saving myself for my husband or wife. I know that with The Christ that I can triumph over every temptation. I choose to live a chaste life because I know that is your will for my life.

My desire is for you to be glorified in me.

In Jesus Name

Amen.

_____   _____
(First and Last name)   (Date)

Notes:

"Marriage, The Commitment That God Purposed To Extend Throughout A Lifetime"

BEFORE YOU SAY I DO: WOMAN

As a single woman there are a few things that you must gain a basic understanding about if you are going to seriously consider marriage. I have listed a few areas that God has helped me with that I am sure will be a blessing to you too. I pray that these areas will constructively help you as you prepare for marriage.

Submission

I am a single, strong willed, vibrant, and independent black woman. There was a time in my life when the word submission and I were like oil and water. We just did not mix! The reason that I struggled with submission is twofold.   First, I was negatively influenced by people who did not live or proclaim the correct biblical meaning of submission. Secondly, I was too immature spiritually to understand the priceless position of power in submission.

For a long time I thought that submission meant less than or weaker than. Simply put submission can be best understood when we look closely at both the prefix and the root part of the word. The prefix *"sub"* means under. The root word *"mission"* means to do; to purse or to perform. So, submission means under the mission of Christ—to do or perform as Christ would perform. We know that the life and teachings of Jesus always demonstrate to us the best way to live.

Actually, in order for a marriage to work both partners have to submit to one another. The bible says submit yourselves one to another in the fear of the Lord (Eph 5:21). Both partners in a marriage should always line up their desires and actions with the word of God.

Marriage is not meant to be a power struggle. Bickering, shouting, and belittling one another will never improve the present circumstance. Behaving that way will only make matters worse. The man is the covering, protector, spokesperson and final authority in the marriage. For the husband is the head of the wife, even as Christ is the head of the church: and he is the Savior of the body (Eph. 5:23).

I know that some of you are saying what about when my husband is wrong? Should I still submit? First I'll say this. You choose whom you submit to so choose a man that loves God and is a doer of His word.

Now lets talk about the power, strength and the priceless position of faith. In Genesis 12:10-20 we see that Abram told a half-truth (lie) that jeopardized his safety, the safety of Sari his wife, and Pharaoh's entire house. Sari was to pose only as Abram's sister. She was his half sister but she was also his wife.

Abram was afraid that The Egyptians would kill him to get Sari so that they could add her to the harem. She was wealthy, beautiful and had potential for being a political alliance. Well, when the Egyptians saw Sari they told Pharaoh about her and she was taken to the palace to be with Pharaoh.

For her sake Abram (*her brother*) was treated well and was given sheep, cattle, donkeys, servants and camels. But the Lord inflicted serious diseases on Pharaoh and his household because Sari was Abram's wife. When Pharaoh found out Sari was Abram's wife he asked them to go but they did not leave empty handed. They left with everything they had originally in addition to everything they had been given.

Abram was wrong but Sari did not *"bad mouth"* her husband. She trusted God. Believe me there are times when, *"silence in golden"*. When we put our faith in God he responds to our faith and his actions speak for us. She was not the weaker one she was in a position of strength because she was being submissive standing not under the strong arm of her husband but willfully pleasing the Lord standing in her faith in God to work things out for the good. The king could have killed them both. However, because Sari was submissive to her husband God protected and blessed both she and Abram. They went into a land of famine and came out of it with much more than they had when they went in.

Help Meet

The wife is responsible for helping her husband. She is not to take over but she is to "*help*" her husband. Helping is not limited to hands on involvement. A wife helps her husbands when she is a constant voice of encouragement and support. As a co-laborer you are to carry your share of the load.   You should do whatever you can do to help him carry out the vision for the marriage. Common interests will help you become more socially compatible but with a common vision you can usher each other into destiny.

Now keep this in mind. If your intended mate has nothing for you to help him do that is not the right mate for you!

Gen 2:18 Now the Lord said it is not good (sufficient, satisfactory) that the man should be alone; I will make him a help meet (suitable, adapted, complementary) for him.

You will be a valuable part of the marriage relationship. "*Help*" in this verse means to supply what the man cannot personally supply. As his wife you will complement not complete your husband and he will do the same for you. "*Meet*" comes from a Hebrew word that means "*opposite*" which means that you should correspond to him. His weakness will be your strengths and your weaknesses will be his strengths.

Femininity+ Sensitivity+ Beauty= Woman

Rejoice in who you are as a woman! We live in an, " *I'm every woman",* society and because of that many men really do not think that women "*want* or *need*" a man. I never have been too excited about the feminist movement. Please, take me out to dinner. Open my door. Pull out my chair. Go ahead and treat me like a woman! Am I capable of doing all those things myself? Yes, but if a man wants to do it, I will gladly allow him the privilege! A man wants to feel needed.

Once I was watching an episode of *Little House On The Prairie* and Albert, a young boy asked a little girl if he could carry her books home from school but the little girl said no. Later in the conversation she insulted Albert because she felt like he was not being a gentleman. He responded, "Well, I was trying to earlier but you would not let me."

Let a man be a man. Men are created instinctively to be protectors, hunters, and providers. Men feel accomplished, successful, and proud when they operate in their God given character. Maybe there is something to the nursery rhyme that says that girls are made of sugar and spice and everything nice! Women are characteristically nurtures, caregivers and receivers. Femininity and sensitivity do not mean weakness. God created women to be beautiful and delicate! That's just who we are created to be and it's awesome!

Believe me, I can relate to being the one who has had to "*do it all*" around the house. As a married woman you will be able to release some of those responsibilities! When you are married to a godly man he instinctively wants to make things easier for you.

1Peter 3:7 (Amp) ....You married men should live considerately with [your wives] with an intelligent recognition of the marriage relation, honoring the woman as [physically] the weaker but realizing that you are joint heirs of the grace (God's unmerited favor) of life, in order that your prayers may not be hindered and cut off. [Otherwise you cannot pray effectively].

Godly husbands will know how relate to their wives with respect, thoughtfulness, perception and finess. Wives to be you must not "*block your blessings*" by not allowing your husband to be the man that God created him to be.

Becoming A Wife

Pro. 18:22. He who finds a [true] wife finds a good thing and obtains favor from the Lord (AMP)

There are three things that can be clearly seen in this verse. The first is that God honors marriage. Favor means to delight. God delights in a man who finds a wife. In this single world in which we live marriage is still a wonderful institution that is blessed and honored by God. Despite the increasing divorce rate marriage really is a terrific thing!

Secondly, the scripture says that a *man* finds a *wife*. I know that this is the twenty-first century but I still think that a man should pursue the woman especially as it relates marriage. Remember, you must allow him be a man!

Thirdly, the man found a *wife*. She was not a wife after marriage but before the marriage. The revelation is this: A woman ought to have some wifely characteristics before the wedding. If you cannot keep order in an apartment living alone then how will you be able to run an entire household that may include not only a husband but children and the family dog. There are some basic skills like meal preparation, laundry, budgeting, time management, and childcare that a woman ought to acquire before marriage.

I must also add that you should not wait and become beautiful just because someone interesting comes along. Do it for you! Do an inventory check! Throw out all those baggy jogging pants, do your hair regularly, put on your pretty face and sweetest perfume everyday! Stop eating off paper plates. Get out the good china and dine alone in style. You will soon see a world of a difference in how much more you appreciate you and your fulfilled days as a single Christian woman.

What you begin before the wedding will not be difficult to maintain after the marriage. If you want your future marriage to be happy, healthy and functional start preparing yourself to be a wife today!

BEFORE YOU SAY I DO: MAN
Commitment

Matt. 25:23...You were faithful with few things, I will put you in charge of many things; enter into the joy of your master

We live in a just do it society where commitment is secondary and fulfilling desire is first priority.   The committed man is the key to a successful family, because the man is the head of the house. If the husband is out of order so goes the family! Therefore, a husband must understand the value of commitment. Commitment is not convenient! Neither is commitment a choice! Commitment means sacrifice. Commitment from the head of the house is absolutely necessary if a family is going to survive. A man is not even eligible for a blessed and joyful marriage if he is not a man of commitment. Take a look at your life now. Are there areas of inconsistency? If you cannot be faithful now over a few things how can you be faithful later over many things?

Name, Honor, Integrity
Pro. 22:1 A good name is more desirable than great riches; to be esteemed is better than silver and gold.

When a man marries a woman in American society the woman takes on the last name of her new husband. Everything that the name represents is now attached to her and all of the children that will be produced from that union. Husbands to be it is very important that the your name be one of honor and integrity because your name not only makes a statement about who you are but it will also make a statement about your family. Your name has both a history and a future.

There are men who have lived most of their lives *"smelling themselves"* and *"sowing oats"* in an attempt to gain the *names* or *labels* that the world wants to award the male gender with like hustler, jock, stud, pimp, mac daddy, babe, and ladies man. At the same time there are men who are worthy of an honorable mention because they have worked diligently to keep a clean record unspotted from the world. These men have a good name.

A name alone can speak volumes. What do you think about when you hear names like Adolph Hitler, Ted Bundy, Jeffery Dahmer, or David Coresh? What about the people who have had to deal with their legacy? Now what comes to mind when you hear names like J.C. Penny, Bill Gates, or Alex Haley? Their names alone bring favor to everyone associated with them!

Man Of Prayer

Daniel 6:7....All the commissioners of the kingdom, the prefects and the satraps the high officials and the governors have consulted together that the king should establish a statue and enforce an injunction that anyone who makes a petition to any God or man besides you, O king, for thirty days, shall be cast into the lion's den.

Now when Daniel knew that the document was signed, he entered his house (now in his roof chamber he had windows open toward Jerusalem) and he continued kneeling on his knees three times a day, praying and giving thanks before his God, as he had been doing previously.
Daniel is described as one who had an excellent spirit. I believe that his excellent spirit had everything to do with his relationship with God. A strong prayer life means a strong relationship with the Lord. Without prayer Daniel could not

have survived the frustrations that went along with being taken captive at the age of about fifteen and living his life in exile.

Without prayer he would not have been able to cope with the uncertainties of living in the foreign land of Babylon where he otherwise would have forgotten God and his identity. Because Daniel was a man of prayer he was still able hear from God in the worst situations for himself and for others, he was favored in the sight of his enemies and he escaped the crisis of the Lion's den.

A strong prayer life will yield an excellent spirit—excellent in spite of the frustrations and uncertainties that inevitably come in the life of a family. Prayer will give you a God-consciousness so that you are aware of the best that God desires for you and the life of your family. Prayer will keep you grounded in who you are because of God and the great potential you have in a life with Him. With a strong prayer life you will be able to hear from God about issues concerning your family and moments that should be as frightening as a lions den will be just like lying among lambs.

Man Of Vision

Pro. 29:18 Where there is no vision the people perish.

As the head of the house you must always have vision. If the head is lifeless with no revelation from God so will the body be as well. A godly man with a vision has the ability to penetrate everyone's spirit in the house with a piece of the same vision that he has received from the Lord. When you have vision you can give direction and encourage others in the house to reach their fullest potential. If you want to be the head of a progressive and fruitful household you must be a man of vision. As the captain of the ship your vision will always lead your family safely to shore.

Communicator

The plain truth is that women generally like to talk more than men. Women are more descriptive about what happens to them. Our general conversation may include the details of our actions and how those actions affected everyone around us.

While men, on the other hand, are generally not as verbal. They feel some things are not worth discussing. One-word responses are often thought adequate enough for them. Wait a minute. Before you jump to biased conclusions. Neither position is better or worse than the other. Men and women are just different.

However men, a woman will feel that she is being ignored and unappreciated if you do not communicate effectively with her. Men, women do not always want you to fix what's wrong sometimes we just want to know that you are listening and that you are trying to understand. I must admit we tend to be like kids sometimes. We think that if we do not make eye contact or if your presence is the other room that your attention is elsewhere. A bit of advice, frantically pressing the remote control buttons is not the best way to show your wife that you are listening.

Men you must learn to be an active listener. Active listening means leaning forward when your mate speaks, maybe holding her hand, nodding your head, and saying things like really, okay, and then what—add to the conversation. Women just want to know that they are being heard. They want to know that you care about how they feel and what is going on in their lives. No matter how insignificant it may seem to you it is a big deal to us.

Husbands to be get ready to share! Women want you to be able to sincerely share how you feel. Men you are going to have to try to talk more! When both of you communicate it eliminates the guessing games, builds trust and develops other avenues of intimacy.

Pro. 31:11-12 The heart of a husband trusts in her confidently and relies on and believes in her securely; so that he has no lack of [honest] gain or need of [dishonest] spoil. She comforts, encourages, and does him only good as long as there is life within her.

Another form of communication is the *"touch"*. I met a married man one time that told me that he made a habit of touching his wife at least five times a day. And these touches did not mean that it was time to jump in the bed, gentlemen! Women like to be noticed. A touch on the shoulder and holding her by the waist as you pass by are excellent ways to communicate to a woman that you are acknowledging her presence. Touch by communication says, your being here means a lot to me.

Amos 3:2 (Amp) Do two walk together except they make an appointment and have agreed?

1.   Do you and the person that intend to marry have a common vision about marriage, children, careers, kingdom building?

2.   What similarities and differences do you share as it relates to budgeting and spending money?

3.   What do you know about your fiancés family?

Pro. 2:11 Discretion shall watch over you, understanding shall keep you.

4.   Have you compared and examined medical histories?

John 8:32b ...the truth shall make you free
5.   Have you both been honest about your past?

6.   How does your intended define the role of both a wife and a husband?

7.   Why do you want to get married? Is that enough? Is that reason good in the sight of God?

2Cor. 3:18 And all of us, with unveild face, [because we] continued to behold [in the Word of God] as in a mirror the glory of the Lord, are constantly being transfigured into His very own image in ever increasing splendor and from one degree of glory to another; [for this comes] from the Lord [Who is] the Spirit.
8.   Are you marrying with the hope of changing your mate? How does individual change come about?

Pro. 25:11 Like apples of gold in settings of silver is a word spoken in the right circumstances.
9.   Is your mate consistently supportive of you emotionally and spiritually? How so?

SS 5:16 His mouth is full of sweetness and he is wholly desirable. This is beloved and my friend.
10.   Is the person that you want to marry a true friend?

2Cor. 6:14 Do not be bound together with unbelievers for what partnership have righteousness and lawlessness, or what fellowship has light with darkness?

1Cor. 3:1-2 And I brethren could not speak to you as to spiritual men, but as to men of flesh, as to infants in Christ. I gave you milk to drink not solid food; for you were not yet able to receive it. In deed, even now you are not yet able.

Eph. 2:10 For we are His workmanship, created in Christ Jesus for good works, which God prepared beforehand so that we would walk in them.

11.   Is your intended eternal mate saved? Is he or she a babe or mature saint? Is he or she active in kingdom building?

Ex. 20:5-6 You shall not worship them or serve them for I the Lord your God am a jealous God, visiting the iniquity of the fathers of the children of the third and forth generations of those who hate me, but showing loving kindness to thousands to those who love Me and keep My commandments.

2Chronicles 7:14 If my people which are called by my name, shall humble themselves and pray and seek my face and turn from their wicked ways, then will I hear from heaven and forgive their sin and heal their land.

12.   What generational curses need to be broken on both sides of the family as it pertains to your, marriage, future family, and individual success?

De. 23:21-23 When you make a vow to the Lord your God, you shall not delay to pay it, for it would be sin in you, and the Lord your God will surely require it of you. However, if you refrain from vowing, it would not be sin in you. You shall be careful to perform what goes out of your lips, just as you have voluntarily vowed to the Lord your God what you have promised.

13.   Could you be committed to that person for the rest of your life? What would or would not prompt you to honor that

commitment?

Ps. 119:105 Thy word is a lamp unto my feet and a light unto my path?
14.   What are your strategies for problem solving?

15.   Is an active social life important to you? What changes will or will not be necessary after marriage? Will the friends that you have now nurture your marriage relationship?

Mark 10:2-12 Some Pharisees came up to Jesus, testing him, and began to question Him whether it was lawful for a man to divorce his wife. And He answered and said to them, "What did Moses command you? They said, "Moses permitted a man to write a certificate of divorce and send her away." But Jesus said to them, "Because of your hardness of hearts he wrote you this commandment. But from the beginning of creation, God made them male and female. For this reason a man shall leave his father and mother and the two shall become one flesh; so they are not longer two, but one flesh. What therefore **God has joined together** let no man separate." (see also Matt. 5:32)
16.   What are your opinions about divorce? Is that an option for you? Do your opinions line up with the will of God?

Pro. 22:7 The rich rules over the poor and the borrower becomes a slave to the lender.
17.   What do you know about your intended mates credit history?

18.   What boundaries or guidelines have been put in place for stepchildren and their parents socially and financially so that your family can be successful and functional?

19.   What undesirable behaviors are you noticing in your relationship now that you are having problems tolerating? Will you be able to deal with those behaviors in marriage?

"MY

GREATEST

ANTICIPATION"

Great Anticipation

John 14: 1-3 Do not let your heart be troubled; believe in God believe also in Me. In my Father's house are many dwelling places; if it were not so, I would have told you; for I go to prepare a place for you. If I go to prepare a place for you, I will come again and receive you to Myself, that where I am, there ye may be also.

At one point or another every Christian will embrace the words in the first verses of the fourteenth chapter of John. In my experience, Christians who read these verses read them in search of strength and encouragement in times of a death of a loved one or in times of distress. The words do wrap around your soul like a soft warm blanket on a cold winter's night. But, these words were also penned to bring us hope of a future life as we reign with The Christ.

As Jesus' final hours on earth were drawing near he comforted the disciples. Jesus told them about His soon coming departure, and the promise of His return so that we can be with He and His Father in a beautiful place called Heaven. When we closely read between the lines we take a glimpse at traditional Jewish culture. Read the verses again and discover a deeper meaning and a delightful revelation.

Jesus often intimately spoke of His relationship with the church likening it to a marriage. Jesus is the bridge groom and the church is the bride. The source of Jesus' comparison is based on a traditional Jewish marriage.

In Jewish culture when a young man was ready to marry, he sought out a suitable wife for him to wed; if his wife had not already been chosen for him. After he had chosen the wife to be, the young man went to visit the father of the bride at the house where his intended bride lived with her family.

The young man would not come to her house empty handed. In order to show his readiness he came bearing gifts for his bride to be. Among the gifts for the bride there would be a journal filled with declarations of his love for his bride to be and the wonderful promises of the future he hoped to share with her.

His proposal and her acceptance began the betrothal period, or espousal as biblical history records. The engagement had officially begun. The eager and excited young man would leave to go and work diligently with his father's help to build and prepare a home for his new bride to be. While the groom was away the bride would often dream of her bridegroom. Although she had not seen him she feel deeply in love with him because she busied herself reading endlessly the journal her bridegroom left, which declared how he would embody the pledge of his love.

The bride waited patiently for her bridegroom to return. She never knew exactly when he would return, although she knew that her groom was coming back very soon. She was certain to keep her lamp ready, filled with oil. She did not want to be caught unaware if he came to get her late during the night.

Now when the fullness of time had surely come, the bride-groom would come unaware, to bring his bride back to the house that he had so lovingly prepared for them to live in. The wedding can begin! It was an intimate celebration with only close family and friends.

I am sure by now that you see the beautiful revelation of how we will be so wonderfully united with our bridegroom Jesus The Christ. We ought to all look forward to that great day in which Jesus, the bridegroom will return for us. We are His glorious church. We are His bride. We should be standing in eager and great anticipation of Beulah, that marriage in the heavens.

Jesus chose us to be His bride. We are now living in our engagement period waiting for the return of our bridegroom. While we eagerly await His return we must continually read His love letter, the written Word that is filled with His precious promises.

When Jesus comes He will take us back with Him to the place that He has prepared just for you and me. Until then we must keep our lamps trimmed with oil always ready to testify of His love. Many will be invited to come and receive His love but few will accept the invitation.

Everyone who has received Him into his or her heart will be there as we celebrate together at the greatest wedding of all time. Single person your bridegroom is coming. Prepare for Him to receive you! Will you be ready when Jesus comes? I am waiting for my King with great anticipation!

Can't wait to see Him—Look upon His face
Bow down before Him thank Him for His grace
Shake hands with the elders the twenty and the four
Say hello to my loved ones who've gone on before
Jesus is preparing a place just for me
If you want to see me in heaven I will be
Time will be my friend the day will never end
Summer winter spring or fall won't have to come at all
I hope to see you there, where all the saints will be,
come and go with me

V. Michael McKay

Notes:

Pastor Deana Gordon is available to minister at your church or upcoming community event!!!
Pastor Deana proclaims the Gospel of the Kingdom that is for all people, and to all people! She ministers to youth, women and men on a wide variety of topics!

For appointments and testimonies contact us at the information line 615-650-8343, send us an e-mail us at progressivelife@msn.com, or write us at P.O. Box 160899 Nashville, TN, 37216.

Order your copy of BROKEN today!

The lives of many have been empowered by the anointed book entitled Broken. Broken is a book that will help you put your past in perspective so that it does not dictate or destroy your future. Skeletons in your closet do not necessarily represent dead issues. Broken is filled with the Word of God that will guide you in facing the tough issues of life. God has a work for you on the other side of the pain. Dwelling in the despair of unpleasant memories of the past will never propel us into the victorious future that God has planned for our lives. Forgiveness, restoration and healing will position us in the place of miracles. Broken leads every reader to a place of confidence and wholeness in the Lord!

BROKEN ORDER FORM Pastor Deana Gordon,
Progressive Life Ministries,
P.O Box 160899 Nashville, TN 37216

****

Name_____

Address_____

_____

Phone Number(s)_____

_____ I am enclosing my offering of $14
(includes $2 s/h) secure my copy for BROKEN.
Return this order form with your check and or money
order payable to:

Progressive Life Ministries

(Please include two phone numbers on all checks. Allow 3-6 weeks
for delivery. Please feel free to make additional copies for those
interested in ordering the book and or becoming a covenant partner!)

Become a Covenant Partner Today!
Become a Partner with this ministry by sowing a one-time $25
seed offering. With this offering you will receive a two
tape series, covenant partner discount card for books,
an official covenant partner certificate and a tape of the month
when we receive your seed for that month!

As a Covenant Partner we ask you to sow a monthly seed offering
as God increases you. We also ask for you to pray for
the ministry regularly. Your offering and prayer will help support
the work of the Kingdom as we impact the world with
the powerful gospel of Jesus the Christ. As a Covenant
Partner the awesome anointing that rest on this ministry will
manifest in your life!! Ministry is possible because of you!

Name/Address_____

TelephoneNumber_____

E-MAIL Address_____

Covenant Partner Offering _____

One Time Seed Offering_____

Thank you! We appreciate YOU!!